MORAL RESPONSIBILITY IN COLLECTIVE CONTEXTS

MORAL
RESPONSIBILITY IN
COLLECTIVE CONTEXTS

Tracy Isaacs

OXFORD
UNIVERSITY PRESS

OXFORD
UNIVERSITY PRESS

Oxford University Press, Inc., publishes works that further
Oxford University's objective of excellence
in research, scholarship, and education.

Oxford   New York
Auckland   Cape Town   Dar es Salaam   Hong Kong   Karachi
Kuala Lumpur   Madrid   Melbourne   Mexico City   Nairobi
New Delhi   Shanghai   Taipei   Toronto

With offices in
Argentina   Austria   Brazil   Chile   Czech Republic   France   Greece
Guatemala   Hungary   Italy   Japan   Poland   Portugal   Singapore
South Korea   Switzerland   Thailand   Turkey   Ukraine   Vietnam

Copyright © 2011 by Oxford University Press, Inc.

Published by Oxford University Press, Inc.
198 Madison Avenue, New York, New York 10016

www.oup.com

Library of Congress Cataloging-in-Publication Data
Isaacs, Tracy Lynn.
Moral responsibility in collective contexts / Tracy Isaacs.
p. cm.
Includes bibliographical references (p.) and index.
ISBN 978-0-19-978296-3 (alk. paper)
1. Responsibility—Social aspects. I. Title.
BJ1461.I82   2011
170—dc22   2010039422

3 5 7 9 8 6 4 2
Printed in the United States of America
on acid-free paper

For my parents, Ray and Norma Isaacs

CONTENTS

CONTENTS

ACKNOWLEDGMENTS

When I began writing this book as a young scholar on my first sabbatical leave in 1998—after having thought about writing it for a couple of years—I expected to have a complete manuscript within the year. But the leave came and went, and though I devoted myself to the project, I did not come close to completing it. Eight years later, at the end of my next sabbatical leave, I had a complete manuscript. Two years later, I submitted a virtually rewritten manuscript in response to the reviewers' comments. When you're with a project for more than a decade, lots of people contribute along the way, from talking through the ideas to reading drafts of chapters, from commenting on work-in-progress at conferences to providing feedback through the formal review process. For all of the contributions my colleagues and friends have made to this work, I am grateful.

My fabulous colleagues in the Moral, Political and Legal Philosophy Research Group at The University of Western Ontario provided consistently helpful feedback on early drafts of many of these chapters. I thank Robert Binkley, Samantha Brennan, Richard Bronaugh, Charles Jones, Dennis Klimchuk, Michael Milde, and

Anthony Skelton for reading and commenting on so much over the years. I have been fortunate to receive incisive comments on written drafts and conference presentations of various chapters from Tavi Black, Neta Crawford, Megan Doney, Jennifer Epp, Sally Haslanger, Violetta Igneski, Diane Jeske, Christine Junge, Brian Lawson, Chris MacDonald, Larry May, and Julia Watt.

I owe special thanks to Christopher Kutz and an anonymous reviewer from Oxford University Press, whose extensive comments on the first draft provided great guidance for improving the final product, and to my colleague Richard Vernon, who read and commented on revised work throughout the process of producing the final manuscript. And I am most grateful to Peter Ohlin, Senior Editor at Oxford, for staying committed and optimistic through the lengthy review process.

The Social Science and Humanities Research Council of Canada (SSHRC) funded the project over a four-year period (1997–2001). Other funding has come from the Dean's Travel and Research Funds in Arts and Humanities, the SSHRC (Internal) International Conference Travel Grant program, and the SSHRC (Internal) Research Grant program, all at The University of Western Ontario. I am fortunate to have experienced two full years of sabbatical leave from the university—1998–99 and 2005–6—during which I worked on the book. The School of Philosophy at the Research School of Social Sciences at Australian National University and the Bunting Institute at Radcliffe College provided me with work space and lively intellectual communities in 1998–99. And what was supposed to be a creative writing residency at the Ucross Foundation in Wyoming (which I had originally planned as a reward for completing the manuscript) supported the final two weeks of revisions in 2009, in idyllic surroundings and a wonderful community of artists. That time was truly a blessing, for which I owe a huge debt of gratitude to Ucross.

As all philosophers know, we make much philosophical progress in discussion periods following the presentation of our work. I thank the following colloquium audiences for wonderful Q and A: the Department of Philosophy, McGill University; the Department of Philosophy, Buffalo State University; the Department of Philosophy, Queen's University; the Department of Philosophy, The University of Western Ontario; the Department of Philosophy, Ryerson University; the School of Philosophy at the Research School of Social Science, Australian National University; the Bunting Institute at Radcliffe College; and the Watson Institute at Brown University. In addition, I thank that following conference audiences: the Twenty-ninth Conference on Value Inquiry, Tulsa, April 2001; Bringing Power to Justice, the University of Western Ontario, April 2003; the North American Society for Social Philosophy, June 2003; the International Society for Social Philosophy and Law, May 2005; the Canadian Philosophical Association, Quebec City in May 2001, Toronto in May 2006, and Saskatoon in May 2007; and the MITing of Minds, Massachusetts Institute of Technology, Cambridge, January 2008.

I thank Ray and Norma Isaacs, Ashley Guindon, Manon Contini, Diane Jeske, Ed Stein, and Gary Smith for encouragement, optimism, and support. Renald Guindon deserves a medal for his many contributions, but will have to settle for heartfelt thanks and my best efforts to return his unconditional love.

Tracy Isaacs
London, Ontario, August 2010

MORAL RESPONSIBILITY IN COLLECTIVE CONTEXTS

INTRODUCTION

1. COLLECTIVE WRONGDOING, COLLECTIVE HARM, COLLECTIVE SOLUTIONS: FOUR CASES

I started to think about writing this book very shortly after the Rwandan genocide in 1994. Over a three-week period in the spring of 1994, over eight hundred thousand members of the Tutsi group and their sympathizers were hacked to death by over one hundred thousand members of the rival Hutu group. The animosity between these two groups flowed directly from a history of Belgian colonialism in Rwanda throughout the twentieth century. Roméo Dallaire, the Canadian general who led the official UN peacekeeping mission in Rwanda during the genocide, writes that "the Belgians viewed the minority Tutsis as closer in kind to Europeans and elevated them to positions of power over the majority Hutu, which exacerbated the feudal state of peasant Hutus and overlord Tutsis."[1] The collective atrocity that escalated into full-scale genocide in the spring of 1994 involved moral failures at the individual and the collective levels. At the collective level, more than the collective agent who perpetrated the act shouldered its share of the collective guilt. When all was said and done, not only were there over one

3

hundred thousand suspected perpetrators, including over sixty-five who have been tried at the International Criminal Tribunal for Rwanda in Arusha, there was also alarming and convincing evidence that the actions of the international community, particularly the United Nations, contributed in great measure to the extent of the slaughter.[2] Despite early reports indicating a coordinated and systematic effort to kill any man, woman, or child who was Tutsi, "as *de facto* custodians of the term 'genocide' the UN was slow to designate the events in Rwanda accordingly."[3]

Not long before the genocide in Rwanda, an official inquiry into the Canadian Red Cross's handling of the Canadian blood supply began. The Commission of Inquiry on the Blood System in Canada, led by Judge Krever and often referred to as "the Krever Inquiry," was convened in response to what has become known as Canada's "tainted blood scandal."[4] This scandal is thought to be Canada's worst public health disaster to date. Through the late 1970s and 1980s, Canada's supply of blood and blood products was contaminated with HIV and hepatitis C. During that time, tainted blood and blood products resulted in two thousand Canadians contracting HIV and sixty thousand becoming infected with hepatitis C; 43 percent of Canada's twenty-three hundred hemophiliacs contracted HIV.[5] The Krever Inquiry raised and attempted to answer questions of responsibility and appropriate compensation, and made recommendations on how to handle the blood supply in the future. Both the Inquiry and, later, the Royal Canadian Mounted Police found organizations and individuals to be responsible for the tainted blood. The Canadian Red Cross has been forever prohibited from having anything to do with Canada's blood supply, has faced many lawsuits from victims seeking compensation, and was charged with criminal negligence.[6]

Until then, my philosophical attention had focused, with the majority of other philosophers interested in responsibility, largely

4

on the metaphysics of individual action and the concept of individual responsibility. Both the genocide in Rwanda and the mishandling of Canada's blood supply for over a decade highlighted for me the need for an effective account of responsibility at the collective level, or at least an account that would make sense of the moral complexities of collective contexts. In neither case would a thoroughly individualistic analysis either of action or of responsibility adequately capture the collective dimensions of the wrong done. To be sure, individuals do not usually escape responsibility in cases of collective wrong, but the scale and complexity of these and other cases render stories of individual responsibility incapable of capturing the full range of responsibility. In Rwanda, for example, though individuals were incited to participate and did so in the tens of thousands, the extensive nature of the genocide reveals it as a collective act, that is, the act of a collective. No one individual can be said to be responsible for the massive atrocity. The presence of collective responsibility in cases such as this does not discount the responsibility of individuals. Not only are individuals responsible for their contributions but also, I argue later, the normative character of individuals' contributions flows in large measure from the collective endeavor of which they are a part. Many morally significant collective action contexts involve a similar normative complexity. In Canada's tainted blood scandal, we see oversights and negligence at the collective level and at the level of individuals who were in positions to make decisions. Focusing only on individuals would not have uncovered the serious systemic difficulties in how Canada's blood supply was administered. Focusing only on organizations such as the Canadian Red Cross, Health and Welfare Canada, and Armour Pharmaceuticals would have allowed individuals who played pivotal contributory roles to walk away blameless. From a normative point of view, neither scenario would have been satisfactory. A two-level theory of moral responsibility, one that recognizes responsibility at the individual and the collective level, is the best and simplest way to capture the structure of responsibility in these cases. The purpose of this book is to develop and defend such a theory.

Since the genocide in Rwanda and the tainted blood scandals in Canada and elsewhere, attention both nationally and globally has turned to more recent events in which we naturally take a collective view: the international response to the events of September 11, 2001; civil war and genocide in Darfur; the war in Iraq; Canada's national apology and the ensuing Truth and Reconciliation Commission for the residential schools program that tore First Nations children from their communities and forced them into residential schools where abuse was rampant. In all of these cases, strong arguments can be made for collective wrongdoing. In none of these cases does collective wrongdoing eclipse individual wrongdoing to the point of erasure. A central goal of my project here is to show that there is normative space for both.

Collective wrongdoing is not the only sort of collective action in which individuals are negatively implicated. In the past decade, awareness of the collective impact humanity is having on the planet Earth has been growing. Public concern for the environment has become mainstream. Even among those who aren't exactly sure what a carbon footprint is, there is increasing consensus that it would be a very good thing for us—for humanity—to reduce the size of the one we're making. What makes this kind of case different from the cases of genocide in Rwanda and the tainted blood supply in Canada is that while the cumulative outcome of our actions constitutes harm, it is less clear whether the harm is the result of collective wrongdoing. There appears not to be a joint or coordinated effort behind the outcome. And if the attribution of negligence requires that someone or some group should have known better, we might not even be able to explain humanity's impact on the environment as resulting from collective negligence. Rather, we are now experiencing the cumulative impact of individuals living their lives in ways that, until recently, no one had good reason to question.

Another area of practice in which collective solutions appear to be needed is the range of social practices that result in oppression. Oppressive social practices, such as social practices of racist or sexist discrimination, often take place in contexts where they are difficult to identify because they have come to be accepted as normal. For example, the earning power of women globally is still far less than the earning power of men globally, and there are patterns indicating systemic wage inequity and lack of opportunity along the lines of race, ethnicity, and class. Individuals' connection to this level of social practice is terribly opaque. What is not so opaque is this: adequately addressing wrongful social practice will require a collective solution.

While the four cases of wrong or harm I have outlined—the Rwandan genocide, the tainted Canadian blood supply, environmental harm, and oppressive social practice—differ from one another in important ways that will receive attention in the chapters to come, they share a demand for a collective analysis and a collective solution. It is this very feature of them and the many cases resembling them that sometimes leads individuals to feel powerless to address them, so enormous do the harms they have wrought seem to be. But as we turn our attention to this feature of them, we can see that it would be a mistake to think that collective action and collective responsibility are of normative interest only in cases of harm or of wrongdoing. Collective solutions are themselves instances of morally significant collective action. Morally praiseworthy collective actions merit our urgent attention, because when individuals see themselves as potentially effective parts of a powerful whole, moral possibilities expand. I take seriously the importance of morally praiseworthy collective action throughout the discussions that follow.

2. TWO LEVELS OF MORAL RESPONSIBILITY

This book has two parts; both engage with questions about responsibility in contexts of collective action. Chapters 1–3 address collective responsibility per se; chapters 4–6 address individual responsibility in collective cases. In part I, I defend collective moral responsibility as an essential level of responsibility, providing normative reasons as well as action-theoretic considerations in support of this position. Philosophers have been and will continue to be attracted to the apparent simplicity of thoroughgoing individualism, thus seeking reductive accounts of collective moral responsibility in which there is, in the end, no real collective moral responsibility. I argue in support of collective moral responsibility, not just as an interesting or efficient conceptual tool or a shorthand placeholder for a set of claims about the responsibility of individuals but, more important, as normatively necessary for adequately understanding collective efforts. In addition to sorting out the theoretical considerations surrounding responsibility in collective contexts, there are more practical reasons for retaining the idea that collectives, not just individuals, can be responsible. I now turn to some of these practical considerations.

Elsewhere, I have argued that when we recognize ourselves as belonging to groups we can see possibilities for change that would not otherwise be apparent.[7] This claim flows from the simple fact that together we can do things that we could not do alone, from moving a grand piano to significantly reducing humanity's carbon footprint. In a later chapter, I address the idea that collective action solutions to global problems are the only ones that will make a difference.[8] In order to enact these solutions, we need to start understanding ourselves in relation to others, as members of communities who can act together as moral agents. Thinking in terms of collective moral responsibility in the form of obligation helps us to see these moral possibilities and to understand our actions as making a difference.

Sometimes people get defensive when urged to think in this collective way because they do not like the implication that they, as individuals, bear some responsibility for the state of the world when their personal contribution appears so minimal as scarcely to make a difference. I deny that being a member of a morally responsible collective necessarily implicates someone morally. Nevertheless, we urgently need to start thinking of ourselves as implicated. An apathy permeates much of what we do; it is grounded in our inability—or perhaps our refusal—to see our actions in the broad context of the actions of others, a context that casts our actions into a wholly new perspective. I maintain that collective moral responsibility, far from diluting the responsibility of individuals, has the potential to influence individuals to take part in collective action and to imagine new possibilities for positive change.

The denial of collective responsibility prevents us, as individuals, from seeing our own moral effectiveness. We can see more possibilities for our own moral effectiveness when we understand our actions in terms of participation in collective ventures. I might think, for example, that what I can donate to cancer research won't make much difference. But when I think of my donation as part of a coordinated fundraising effort, its significance changes. From the point of view of an individual moral agent, "every little bit counts" only when we can see that others with whom we are acting together are also doing something. Think of some small part of a machine. If we take it out, it is useless on its own. The part only makes a difference when it is working in concert with the other parts. When each part is doing its job, the whole thing works. It is very important for individual moral agents to understand themselves as playing possibly small, but certainly valuable, parts. When individuals think of their actions in this way, moral possibilities expand.

Thinking in terms of collective moral responsibility can also open up the moral possibilities that individuals see for themselves through the mechanism of collective moral obligation. I maintain that collective obligation lends shape and form to the obligations of individuals. When we do not see ourselves as members of collectives that are capable of action, it is easy to ignore or overlook moral obligations that we, in fact, have. We see this frequently in individual responses to the suffering of others. Overwhelmed by the magnitude of global suffering, individuals believe they cannot make meaningful contributions: "If I can't make a difference, then I don't have to do anything," someone might think, applying modus tollens to "ought implies can." But if collective obligation actually mediates individual obligation—as I argue it does[9]—then understanding ourselves as members of collectives does not just make us aware of moral possibilities, it can also make us aware of moral obligations. Given the way collective obligations shape the obligations of individual members of collectives, it is a mistake to think that there is no interaction between the collective and individual levels of agency. Where collective action would clearly make a moral difference, we shall see how collective obligations help to organize and give form to individual obligations and hence to individual moral responsibility.

Moreover, the potential for joint action deserves recognition as a positive force in a troubled world. The more we see ourselves as members of effective groups that could make a difference, the more hope there is for moral progress in the world. The simple observation that together people can achieve what no individual could do alone is profound and significant.

Of course, there is a dark side to this observation. Groups of people can be powerful forces of evil as well as good. Indeed, much of the interest moral philosophers and others have in understanding collective action and collective moral responsibility stems from the power of collectives to engage in wrongful and blameworthy undertakings. We have seen and continue to see examples of collective moral wrong, such as genocide, that would not have been possible without individuals acting together. In those cases, the framework I develop helps us to understand the magnitude of the collective wrong as flowing from collective intentions and collective actions. Furthermore, there is no denying that the individual contributions are part of something larger, and that their being embedded in blameworthy collective actions means that they are themselves blameworthy in a particular and morally significant way that cannot be articulated independently of the collective action context in which they participate. This consequence of my analysis casts sharply into focus why participation in collective wrongs is blameworthy at the individual level. There is no collective cloak to shield people when they are contributing members to collective wrongdoing.

The view I propose in the following chapters articulates why both the collective and the individual levels of moral responsibility are normatively required. At the same time, I recognize and in some measure demystify the metaphysical and normative complexity in the relationship between the collective and individual levels of action and responsibility. My approach dispenses with common misconceptions about collective guilt and draws attention, particularly in the later chapters, to the multiplicity of ways that collective contexts can affect moral responsibility at the level of individuals. Collective contexts do not just create conditions of collective moral responsibility; as my discussion shows, there is interplay between collective wrong and individual responsibility, between collective obligation and individual obligation, and between cultural context and individual responsibility.

3. THEORETICAL BACKGROUND

The central thesis of this book is that there are two distinct levels of moral responsibility: the individual level and the collective level. I claim that an adequate understanding of moral responsibility requires attention to both. Much philosophical work has been done that focuses on one or the other. I contend that this approach will inevitably leave out an area of normative significance, resulting in an incomplete account of moral responsibility. Most philosophical discussions about individual moral responsibility sidestep consider-ations of the collective features of situations in which individuals act. This narrow focus on individual responsibility sometimes erases from view normatively significant act descriptions. Act descriptions that articulate collective content can reveal morally sig-nificant information about individual actions. For example, a murder that takes place as part of a genocide is, if it fulfills certain criteria, not only a murder even if "murder" is among the morally relevant descriptions of it.[10] The invisibility of these ways of describing and understanding the acts of individuals leaves us ill-equipped to deal with individual moral responsibility in some important cases. The insight worth highlighting here, and that will be developed in due course, is that an adequate account of collective moral responsibility grounds accurate moral evaluations not just of collectives but also of individuals.

I now turn to an explanation of some background of how I understand moral responsibility, how it differs from legal and causal responsibility, and what makes agents responsible.

Let me state very generally how I understand moral responsibility and the way it is different in kind from causal and legal responsibility. I want also to explain the distinction between moral responsibility, understood as an evaluative concept, and moral responsibilities, understood as another way of describing our duties or obligations.

Moral responsibility is the blameworthiness and praiseworthiness of moral agents. It differs from causal responsibility in a number of ways. First, moral agents can be morally responsible and causally responsible, whereas nonmoral agents, inanimate objects, forces of nature, and events can only be causally responsible. An avalanche may be causally responsible for a number of deaths, but the avalanche is neither blameworthy nor praiseworthy. Second, though causal responsibility frequently accompanies moral responsibility, it does not always. Usually, if I am blameworthy for something, then my actions caused it. So, for example, consider a situation in which you loan me your car and I return it as a write-off. There might be circumstances in which I am blameworthy for the damage to your car even though I was not the driver. For example, upon getting the car from you I in turn might have given the keys to my teenaged son, who then drove your car into a tree. In this case, his actions caused the car's condition, but I am blameworthy to the extent that you entrusted the vehicle to my care. Third, there are cases in which agents may be causally responsible for something without being blameworthy. Excuses and accidents are two scenarios in which causal responsibility and moral responsibility come apart from each other. Accidental heroics, in which someone inadvertently saves the day, are another example. Praise is not in order in cases such as these. In short, causal responsibility has no necessary normative implications. Moral responsibility is essentially normative in nature, insofar as it is an agent's blameworthiness or praiseworthiness for her or his morally significant actions.

Moral responsibility is also different from legal responsibility, though both have normative features and there is some overlap between them. Legal responsibility flows from a legal system, and legal systems "recognize, create, vary and enforce obligations."[11] The main differences between moral and legal responsibility are in the range of objects for which one is responsible in each respective domain and in the enforceability of the associated obligations. In the moral domain, I am morally responsible, that is, blameworthy, when I tell a lie in order to borrow a friend's car, but I am not legally guilty of anything. Similarly, I might be legally responsible, that is, guilty of a violation, if I do not stay for the duration of the long red light on a deserted country road in the middle of the night, but I am not blameworthy in any moral sense. These are familiar examples of the ways the moral and the legal cover some different territory. With respect to enforceability, law enforcement systems ensure that there are consequences for wrongdoers who are caught violating laws. Morality, however, has no comparable coercive systems in place (notwithstanding the power of peer pressure in the form of censure or praise).

In addition to these differences, legal responsibility suggests a different understanding of "responsibility." Instead of being evaluative, legal responsibility is more closely associated with our obligations and duties as dictated by a relevant legal system. We have certain legal responsibili*ties* according to that system. Sometimes, when discussing morality, we understand responsibility in this way, too. We are morally responsible, that is, morally required, obligated, or duty bound, to tell the truth and to refrain from harming. This is quite different from the normative-evaluative sense of moral responsibility that is my focus. While moral responsibility, in the sense of blameworthiness and praiseworthiness, is a function of how well or badly we fulfill our moral responsibilities, these are distinct senses of moral responsibility; running them together can create confusion. Whether agents are blameworthy or praiseworthy is a separate question from what morality requires of them in terms of duties and obligations. Unless I indicate otherwise, I use "moral responsibility" in the former, not the latter, sense. I now turn to a brief discussion of my assumptions concerning the features of responsible moral agents and the nature of praise and blame.

Responsible agents are sometimes blameworthy and sometimes praiseworthy for their actions. They are members of the moral community and, in virtue of that membership, there are normative constraints on what, morally speaking, they may permissibly do. I assume that most of us are morally responsible agents because we are capable of intentional actions, that is, we are able to act on the basis of reasons. Praise and blame function as normative evaluations of agents and their actions. Some philosophers have a consequentialist understanding of praise and blame, according to which these function primarily as tools for good behavior. This is not my view; though we might well act in particular ways in order to win praise, this is not the normative purpose of praise. Traditionally, philosophical discussions of moral responsibility have turned on questions of free will and determinism at the level of individuals. Philosophers have supposed that without free will, choice, the ability to act on the basis of reasons, control, or some adequately constrained ability to do otherwise, it would be illegitimate to consider people morally responsible for their actions.[12] But the deterministic view of the world that dominates modern thought says that prior states and the laws of nature fully determine the state of world at any given time.[13] For this reason, determinism threatens our understanding of ourselves as moral agents, suggesting the disturbing possibility that we are operating under the illusion, not the reality, of choice. Philosophical discussions of free will and determinism tread a well-worn and worthy path articulating the problem's proper formulation, its solution—whether compatibilist or libertarian—and its gravity (or lack thereof). I leave the problem of determinism, if it is a problem, in the capable hands of others so that I may turn to a set of issues that arises when we think about moral responsibility in collective contexts.

4. COLLECTIVE CONTEXTS AND MORAL RESPONSIBILITY

My project is not alone in departing from the persistently individualistic focus of traditional discussions about responsibility. Since the mid-twentieth century, philosophers have recognized that moral responsibility is not simply about specifying a set of capacities in individuals.[14] It is also about understanding how the actions of one moral agent can interact with those of others in both loosely structured and highly organized collective scenarios, thereby changing the nature of individuals' actions and the consequences of those actions in morally significant ways. When individuals act together, they bring about outcomes—good or bad—that cannot be achieved without a combined effort. Consider, for example, the collective response to the Southeast Asian tsunami at the end of 2004. The coordinated efforts of individuals who made donations, government matching programs, and relief agencies that received the donations and provided a range of services from rescue operations to programs to reunite families made a difference in a way that individuals acting independently could not. The collective response was praiseworthy, and the people who contributed to it were praiseworthy because of their contributions to the overall effort. This example helps to illustrate that collective action is a significant context for understanding moral responsibility of individuals and helps to advance our understanding of the moral responsibility of collectives.

Philosophers who attend to collective moral responsibility investigate, among other issues, the question of under what conditions, if any, it is possible to consider collective entities to be morally responsible agents. Views about collective responsibility range from the claim that it does not exist[15]—that collectives cannot be responsible because they are not the right sorts of entities to qualify as moral agents—to the claim that some collectives, particularly but not only highly organized collectives such as corporations, can be morally responsible.[16] But just as discussions of individual responsibility have overlooked the significance of the collective, most discussions of collective moral responsibility either pass over individual responsibility or deal with it badly. They pass over it by remaining entirely focused on responsibility at the collective level. Peter French, for example, has done important and influential work that emphasizes that corporate structures, policies, and decision procedures, not the intentions of individuals acting within corporations, ground corporate agency.[17] According to his account, the moral responsibility of corporations is not related to, nor does it help us to determine, the moral responsibility of individuals acting within them. This is not a fault of the view, but it does mean that individual moral responsibility is not at all addressed in French's discussion. Silence about individual responsibility is one of the main reasons French's collectivist view has faced so much criticism.

I pay careful attention to the impact of collective contexts on the responsibility of individuals, while at the same time addressing collective responsibility.

Typically, when individual responsibility arises in discussions of collective responsibility, it is in one of two ways. The first way is in the claim that collective moral responsibility threatens to dilute or completely absorb individual responsibility, letting individuals off the hook when they are actually accountable.[18] This bodes ill for collective moral responsibility, since most people—myself included—think that in many cases individual agents who participate in collective wrongdoing are blameworthy for so participating. The second way individual responsibility arises is in the claim that collective moral responsibility is illegitimate because it holds some individuals responsible for the acts of others.[19] Proponents of this view use it as a reductio against the very idea of bona fide collective moral responsibility. This may well be the most important objection to collective moral responsibility, and I address it at length in chapter 2.

I show that neither of these consequences for individual moral responsibility follows from an adequate account of collective moral responsibility. Individuals would only be absolved of individual responsibility for their part in collective action if an attribution of collective moral responsibility necessarily exhausted all of the responsibility in a given case. The view I develop, in which I defend the individual and collective as two distinct levels of moral responsibility, does not entail that collective moral responsibility dilutes individual moral responsibility in any way. The reason for this is that collective moral responsibility is blameworthiness or praiseworthiness of a collective, whereas individual moral responsibility is blameworthiness or praiseworthiness of an individual. The concern that collective moral responsibility holds some moral agents responsible for the acts of others arises from the supposition that an attribution of collective moral responsibility entails that every member of the responsible collective is responsible as an individual. This does not follow from my view, where collective moral responsibility is understood as operating on a level distinct from individual moral responsibility. Individual moral responsibility is not a function of collective moral responsibility (or vice versa) and claims about the responsibility of collectives do not entail (or erase) claims about the responsibility of individual members. Gaining clarity on this point helps to address the most persistent worry about collective moral responsibility and to deny that worry's adequacy as a reason for rejecting the possibility that collectives may be responsible.[20]

5. HOPE

Let me end the introduction by saying that I hope readers will see hope in these pages. The two-level analysis is meant not only to provide an account that I believe makes sense of moral responsibility in collective contexts but also to point to ways that we might alter our self-understandings so that we see ourselves as effective members of collective bodies—some of which may be agents and some of which may be potential agents, but all of which have a powerful impact on the world through their intentional actions. Although an important part of the project is to provide a framework for thinking about blame and praise for deeds already done, it also articulates ways of understanding how we might turn our attention forward to seek and perform solutions to some of the global challenges facing us today. As individuals we understandably feel small and powerless when we think about climate change and oppression, for example.

But when we reorient ourselves in relation to others and take the broader perspective of collective action, new moral possibilities present themselves, and our contributions, small though they may be, gain greater significance from the collective contexts in which they take place.

PART ONE

COLLECTIVE MORAL RESPONSIBILITY

[1]

INTENTIONAL COLLECTIVE ACTION

My main interest in collective action contexts is normative. I advocate a two-level theory of moral responsibility in which there is moral responsibility at both the individual and the collective levels. The normative conclusions I wish to establish rest on the claim that intentional action also operates on two levels, the individual and the collective. I understand intentional collective action as the intentional action of collective agents. In this chapter, I outline my view of collective agency by distinguishing between two types of collective agents—organizations and goal-oriented collectives—and giving an account of their respective intentional structures. My purpose is to establish that collectives may have intentions and are capable of intentional action.

Where moral agency is concerned, we can roughly distinguish between two species of views, those of the individualists and those of the collectivists. Individualists believe that agency and responsibility are ascribable only to individual human agents and that claims about collective agency and collective responsibility are reducible to claims about the agency and responsibility of individuals. Collectivists subscribe to a less reductionist and more holistic view, arguing that claims about collective agency and responsibility do not reduce to claims about the agency and responsibility of individuals.

My view is collectivist. For both action-theoretic and normative reasons, I claim that collective agency and collective moral responsibility operate at a different and indispensable ontological and explanatory level from individual agency and individual moral responsibility. According to my view, claims about collective moral responsibility neither entail nor are derivable from claims about individual moral responsibility. Furthermore, collective intentions, from which the agency of collectives derives, are not simply collections of individual intentions, and collective actions are not simply collections of individual actions. Collective actions are the products of the intentions of collectives. My goal in this chapter is to explain my account of collective agency. I begin with a brief discussion of types of collectives.

1.1 TYPES OF COLLECTIVES

Collectives range in type from highly structured entities, of which corporations are the paradigmatic example, to loosely structured groups of as few as two people. The number of members a collective has is not necessarily an indication of its complexity or simplicity. Large groups, such as rioting mobs, might have little or no structure; small groups, such as a department of philosophy, might have a quite complex structure outlined in a formal constitution and well-defined administrative roles and responsibilities. The more structure a collective has, the easier it is to dissociate its identity from any particular cohort of members, though structure is not the only consideration when it comes to such dissociation. Highly structured collectives, which I call *organizations*, are the most obvious and least contestable candidates for moral agency. Corporations, nonprofit groups, nations, universities, departments of philosophy, and professional sports teams are all examples of organizations. Of the four examples I outlined in my introduction, only one—the Canadian Red Cross—clearly falls into this category. The perpetrators of genocide in Rwanda, contributors to global warming, and participants in oppression are not clearly members of organized groups. If the Rwandan genocide was perpetrated by a collective, it was not a collective we can rightly call an organization. The reason we cannot is that although there was a common goal and a coordinated effort, there was not an organizational structure of the sort possessed by the collective that perpetrated the Holocaust.

A different kind of collective from an organization, one that fits the profile of the collective that perpetrated the Rwandan genocide, coalesces around action toward the achievement of a particular joint goal. I call this kind of collective a *goal-oriented collective*. It is important that the goal be a joint goal, the obtaining of which requires, or at least is pursued through, collective action. Goal-oriented collectives do not need to be as enormous as the one that perpetrated the Rwandan genocide. Two people going for a walk together, three people painting a house together, a thousand people doing the wave at a sports event, or tens of thousands of people "Running for the Cure" all constitute goal-oriented collectives.

What are we to say of my other two examples: those who contribute to global warming and those who participate in oppressive social practice? It is not the case that these examples point to an organization. There is no structured collective entity of which contributors to global warming or participants in oppression are members. Nor does it seem accurate to say that they qualify as goal-oriented collectives. The cases both lack a joint goal around the achievement of which a group comes together in solidarity. Yet both of these cases have a great deal of moral significance: the first points to a mounting harm of potentially earth-destroying proportions; the second to a class of cases involving systemic injustice. I claim that the collective contexts of these cases are important in the determination of individual moral responsibility. As described, they do not, however, identify or isolate collective entities to which we might ascribe agency. Global warming might be best construed as a harmful cumulative consequence of noncoordinated parallel actions. As such, it might well generate collective and individual obligations. I argue as much in chapter 5. But as a consequence of parallel actions, we have no moral or ontological reasons on the basis of which to attribute it to a collective entity. In the case of oppression, it is tempting to attribute its existence to the behavior of privileged social groups, the members of which are usually beneficiaries of practices of discrimination against others. For example, some like to condemn wealthy white North Americans, especially men, for systemic injustice against the poor or women or members of nonwhite racial groups. I hesitate to identify these kinds of groups as agents. There are compelling arguments, well-represented in feminist scholarship, detailing the importance of recognizing the complex network of privilege and disadvantage at work in oppressive social contexts—we are all members of a multiplicity of social groups, some of which define our privilege, others of which yield disadvantage.[1] Identities are, above all, intersectional.[2] Carving out social groups on the basis of categories that typically delineate privilege and disadvantage is not, therefore, an especially helpful way of isolating collective entities. For this reason, I do not address social groups as such in my analysis of collective responsibility and collective agency. My view does not, however, require that they not exist. It is consistent with my view that within types of collectives we might include the rough category of *aggregates*. Aggregates are collections of people that are grouped together because they share some common characteristic. We can think of *social groups* as a subcategory within aggregates. Later on, I return to this idea of aggregates when I consider what sorts of collective obligations might exist for addressing seemingly insurmountable global problems such as global warming, oppression, poverty, and starvation.[3]

The final type of collective entity, which I mention only to set aside, is the type that is nothing more than a mereological sum. A mereological sum is the notional composite of any random collection of things, not necessarily connected in time or space or in any principled way around any purpose and not organized by any structural features or common characteristics. I, my third-grade teacher, and the queen of Denmark are an example. There are no candidate features in a mereological sum of this kind to suggest agency, though of course it is possible that I, my third-grade teacher, and the queen of Denmark could come together as a goal-oriented collective.

The foregoing discussion establishes that with respect to the four examples I outlined in my introduction, the Red Cross is an example of an organization, the perpetrators of the Rwandan genocide are an example of a goal-oriented collective, and the cases of global warming and oppression are examples of morally significant collective contexts but not of collective entities that exhibit collective agency.

Organizations and goal-oriented collectives share a common feature in virtue of which they have agency: a collective intentional structure that gives rise to collective intention and collective action. Their intentional structures qualify them as moral agents insofar as the structures enable them to act intentionally. It is worth noting that the claim that moral agency rests on the capacity to act intentionally does not require that agents are responsible only when exercising that capacity. Much as rational agents have the capacity to act rationally even when acting irrationally, moral agents are capable of acting intentionally even when they are not. Thus, while the capacity for intentional action is important to account for moral agency, the scope of moral agency goes beyond those cases in which agents are acting intentionally. This distinction is important for explaining how some agents are responsible for negligence or omissions. These sorts of cases often involve behavior that is not intentional.

There are notable differences between the intentional structures of organizations and those of goal-oriented collectives. Because organizations are highly structured and have many features that are relevant to their agency that goal-oriented collectives lack, I address them separately in the discussion that follows. While some might prefer to seek a uniform account, I believe that organizations and goal-oriented collectives are sufficiently different in their intentional structures that nothing is gained by a uniform account. Indeed, there is a much sharper separation between the intentions of individuals within an organization and the intentions of the organization itself than is the case in goal-oriented collectives. And collective goals and individuals' intentions to contribute to the achievement of those goals play an important structural role in collective intentions in goal-oriented collectives.

I begin with organizations.

1.2 THE INTENTIONAL STRUCTURE OF ORGANIZATIONS

How are we to understand the claim that the Canadian Red Cross failed to adequately screen the blood supply between 1980 and 1990? Understanding the Canadian Red Cross as an organization, we can assume structures in which the organizational roles and authority structures are outlined and the organization's policy—including its mission and goals, as well as procedures for making organizational decisions and for the organization taking action—is articulated. The most familiar articulation of this idea may be attributed to Peter French in his widely read account of corporate internal decision structures.[4]

These structures yield a level of intentional action that is distinct from the intentional action of the individuals who perform their organizational roles. The collective level is distinct, insofar as the organization's actions flow from its intentions. The individuals' actions flow from their intentions, and their intentions are not constitutive of the intentions of the organization, even if the individuals' actions are at least partly constitutive of the organizations' actions. In the organization case, there is a sharp disconnect between the individuals' and the collective's intentions (much sharper than in the goal-oriented collective case, as will shortly be explained).

French's original observation concerning corporate intention has great staying power: "when the corporate [organizational] act is consistent with, an instantiation or an implementation of corporate [organizational] policy, then it is proper to describe it as having been done for corporate [organizational] reasons, as having been caused by a corporate [organizational] desire coupled with a corporate [organizational] belief and so, in other words, as corporate [organizational] intentional."[5] The most significant feature of this analysis is that in order to understand the organizational intention there is no need to refer to the intentions of individuals. The content of their intentions is entirely beside the point. If organizational decisions are taken in the form of votes on motions, for example, it may well be that individuals whose roles require them to participate in the decision cast their votes on the basis of personal reasons. Nonetheless, the decision is the organization's intention, irrespective of individuals' reasons for voting as they do. The collective action that follows is the product of the collective's intention. It is theoretically possible that an organization might intentionally pursue a course of action that is not the action that anyone in the organizational structure intended that the organization pursue. Compromise is frequently the rule in group decision-making, mandating courses of action that would not be pursued if any one individual were in a position to make an executive decision. Even in cases in which an individual is authorized to make executive decisions, such that this individual's decisions are the organization's, the decisions she or he makes qua the organizational role are not always consistent with decisions that would reflect the pursuit of her or his personal interests. The artistic director of the Stratford Theatre Festival might, for example, have carte blanche to select the full slate of plays for the next season. Assume she has a low opinion of Broadway musicals and would not include them at all if she were at liberty to stage only what she liked. Nonetheless, the festival intends to run at least two such productions each season. They always sell out, and it is part of the festival's mission to offer a mix of Shakespearean productions and more accessible, crowd-pleasing works, recognizing that there is not always overlap between these two categories. The director's executive decision is constrained by the goals and mandate of the organization that is the theatre company regardless of the personal tastes of the artistic director. The decision the artistic director makes may legitimately be redescribed as the festival's decision. However, the director's intentions at the individual level are not redescribable as those of the festival.

In this analysis of the intentional structure of organizations and the manner in which it gives rise to collective action, I have avoided speaking about joint goals and collective projects. The reason for this is that where organizations are concerned it is a mistake to link the analysis of action too closely to the intentions and goals of individuals, whether jointly or individually held. As the previous example showed, organizational action might result when people are simply performing their roles. They do not need to share any big-picture commitment to the overall goals of the collective. Many who work in institutional settings do not have any sense of invest-ment in what the institution is about, yet as they perform their roles their actions contribute to the actions of the organization. Requiring commitment to a shared goal overstates what is required for collec-tive action to take place in an organization. The policies, procedures, mission, role definition, and structures of authority are what pro-duce intentional action in these settings. Particular members might be completely alienated from the collective goals—perhaps they perform their function just for the paycheck or because they enjoy exercising the specific skills required by their job—yet their actions within their roles might be constituents of the collective actions of the organization.

I have not claimed that the actions of organizations do not require individuals' participation in order to take place. Collective actions would not happen if individuals did not perform their roles according to the relevant structures. Nonetheless, organizations' intentional structures are distinct from the intentions of the indi-viduals performing their functions within those structures. The structural features of organizations make them the clearest collec-tive candidates for moral agency.

Organizations are not, however, the only types of collective en-tities to which moral responsibility may legitimately be attributed. Because goal-oriented collectives lack the highly structured charac-ter of organizations, an analysis of their intentional structures cannot invoke many of the important constituents of organizations. None-theless, goal-oriented collectives do have the capacity for intentional action. I turn to an explanation of intentional agency in these less-structured collectives.

1.3 THE INTENTIONAL STRUCTURE OF GOAL-ORIENTED COLLECTIVES

Recall that a goal-oriented collective is a collective whose members come together around the achievement of a particular goal. That goal might be long or short term. Its achievement might involve significant planning or virtually none. The collective might have very many members or just two. The perpetrators of the Rwandan genocide were a goal-oriented collective; you and I making dinner together are a goal-oriented collective. In recent years, the majority of the philosophical literature about collective, joint, or shared intention and action has had what I am calling goal-oriented collectives as its focal point. One reason for this focus is the recognition that many cases of collective action that appear to merit moral analysis do not involve highly structured organizations. Another reason for this focus is that the relevant collective actions lend themselves quite readily to an individualist analysis. A number of theorists maintain, for example, that the relevant locus of analysis for these sorts of collective endeavors—from a two-person case of going for a walk together to a many-person case of genocide—is individual intention.[6] Some individualists propose to locate the collectivity in the content of individual intention—in the commitment to a joint goal or the individual's intention to participate in the collective action aimed at achieving the goal. Under this analysis, a collective intention is not the intention of a collective entity but rather an individual's intention, albeit one with collective content.[7] If the analysis stopped there, individual intentional agency would be the only real agency there is, and any meaningful attributions of moral responsibility would remain at the level of individuals. These accounts are instructive, but I do not believe the analysis should stop there. Rather, we should understand the collective intentions of goal-oriented collectives as the collectives' intentions.

In recent contributions, several philosophers have offered what I consider hybrid views, in the sense that they claim their views to be in some ways collectivist or holistic and in other—perhaps more fundamental—ways individualist or reductionist. Christopher Kutz, for example, offers a version of explanatory reductionism about collective action that he notes is compatible with "moderate forms of holism." He himself subscribes to one such moderate form of holism, according to which he denies that "a full explanation of collective action can be given without reference to collectives or social facts, because reference to irreducibly holistic facts and entities must occur in an account of the mental states of individual agents."[8] While collectivist or holistic in this respect, Kutz's view relies on the individualist notion of a participatory intention, that is, an individual's intention to do her or his part in a collective act. The content is in an important respect collective, but the intention itself is not the intention of a collective. Kutz draws explicit attention to this individualistic basis as one of the attractive features of his theory. Another hybrid view comes from Seumas Miller, who distinguishes between "the *logical* priority of individual actions over joint actions" and the, at times, explanatory priority of collective ends and interests.[9] Collective ends might contribute causally to the formation of individual ends and motivations. Thus, Miller identifies himself as being "in some sense" a holist and notes, further, that his view is "collectivist in complexion" because it acknowledges that both individual and collective activity depend in significant ways on social forms. For all that, Miller's theory is fundamentally individualist, insofar as the central analytical concept, the collective end, is an individualist notion; a collective end is a species of individual end that "exists only in the heads of individual agents."[10] Finally, Raimo Tuomela draws a distinction between conceptual and ontological issues, noting that his theory "is conceptually rather anti-individualistic, even if ontologically it is, if not individualistic, at least interrelationistic and eschews collective agents and actions in a literal ontological sense."[11] He maintains that "in this account, a group is viewed as a collectively constructed agent that can have goals, beliefs, and so on and that can act, although that is not literally true."[12] Of the three views I have noted as hybrid, Tuomela's instantiates the most liberal blending of seemingly irreducibly collective notions (particularly joint intentions characterized by the "we-mode") and the assertion that none of this elaborate apparatus should be taken as literal.

I enter this discussion committed to a more collectivist than hybrid view; I see no reason to deny the reality of goal-oriented collectives as agents with intentional structures resulting in collective action. They are different, however, from organizations. My purpose is to render plausible the idea that goal-oriented collectives have intentions and intentional structures that transcend the intentions and intentional structures of their members.

We should think about goal-oriented collectives as unities of a special kind. Insofar as the whole is greater than the sum of the parts, we might consider them to be organic unities or organic wholes. One reason for thinking this is simple physical possibility: together we can perform actions we cannot perform alone. I cannot go for a walk together alone. I cannot play street hockey alone. I cannot perform orchestral works alone. Only collectives can be the agents of these actions. Where goal-oriented collectives are concerned, their goals are fundamentally joint. For example, doing the wave at a sports event requires the cooperation of many others, all of whom share the goal.[13] Beyond physical possibility, we need also to recognize that pooling our resources does not just create possibilities for coordination. In many cases, our interactions take us places where no one of us would even think to go alone. For example, two people

writing a paper together, as a group, might well end up with a conclusion that neither would have devised on her or his own. Their
collective effort yields a result quite different from what they would
have come up with independently of each other. A more elusive but
arguably significant feature of collectives is the quality of the "chem-
istry" among the members. Any teacher who has taught the same
course several times knows that in some years it is a great success,
whereas in others it falls flat. This has less to do with any particular
member of the class than with how the members combine. One year
the class is energetic and enthusiastic. The following year's group is
lethargic and introverted. The goal is the same, but different collectives have different characters or personalities. In addition to these
considerations, there are facts about identity and endurance through
changes of membership. Many goal-oriented collectives—for
example the perpetrators of the Rwandan genocide, the people who
do the wave at a sports event, or the participants in the "Run for the
Cure" fundraiser for breast cancer research—have the capacity to
withstand significant changes in membership without their identities being compromised. If there is a strong wave going around the
stands and I decide to sit it out when it comes to my section because
I am playing with my new smart phone, there is no good argument
for establishing that it is a different wave from the one it would have
been if I had participated. The success of a particular instantiation of
the wave phenomenon does not stand or fall with the participation
of any particular contributor. I make these points as a means of
suggesting that goal-oriented collectives are in several ways more
than the sum of their parts. This thesis does not require the absurd
claim that the parts are irrelevant. It requires only that the manner in
which the parts come together is as significant as the parts themselves. I do not believe this way of understanding this kind of collective amounts only to a useful fiction or should be thought of

conceptually as merely a manner of speaking. It has metaphysical substance sufficient to ground moral agency.

1.3.1 Collective Intention in Goal-Oriented Collectives

I favor an understanding of collective intention as a state of affairs consisting of a complex of appropriately constrained individual intentions, the relationships between them and to the joint goal, and the individuals' understanding of themselves as standing in relation to others as members of a group in pursuit of a joint goal. Understood this way, the collective intention has independent standing that may, in some cases, constrain how individuals may legitimately participate in the collective activity. Michael Bratman suggests that a shared intention consists "primarily of a web of attitudes of the individual participants"[14] and I concur with the gist of this idea. Nonetheless, our respective views rest on different sides of the individualist/collectivist divide. Bratman understands himself to be offering a view that is "broadly individualistic in spirit."[15] I consider my account to be more collectivist, both in spirit and in substance. The relations between individuals' intentions and the way individuals understand themselves as standing in relation to others as members of a group are essential features of collective intentions, without which the collective action would not come about. Just as the collectives themselves ought to be understood along the lines of organic unities, so should their intentions be understood similarly. They flow from the collectivity of the collective. They are not simply aggregates of individual intentions. The way the individual intentions combine and the way members of groups understand themselves as members of groups give rise to collective intentions that, in turn, result in collective actions. It would be a mistake to think of this view as reductionistic or as individualistic. It recognizes the collective level as a different, though dependent, level of action.

Furthermore, this view does not require that the intentions of goal-oriented collectives are collective mental states or states of consciousness, any more than the intentions of organizations are these things. Some deny collective intentions on the grounds that intentions must be mental states. If that were the case, then the very idea of collective intentions would require a collective mind to house them. For example, Miller claims that intentions must exist in the heads of agents.[16] This gives him an easy way to deny the existence of truly collective intentions: since collectives do not have heads in which intentions may exist, there are no collective intentions. Alternatively, however, we may understand collective intentions as states of affairs, identifiable in part by their functional roles.[17] As long as they function at the collective level of action in the same way that individual intentions function at the level of individual action, then we may think of them as intentions.

The first element in the analysis of collective intentional action in goal-oriented collectives is the collective goal. The collective goal is simply the end at which the collective aims. The conception of a collective goal necessarily includes reference to its being intended, because there are no collective goals in the abstract, dissociated from the collective that intends to bring them about. For example, when we intend to make dinner together, our collective goal is to make dinner together; when the audience at the hockey game intends to do the wave, the collective goal is to do the wave; when a group of people intends to commit genocide, the collective goal is to destroy a particular ethnic, racial, or religious group because of their ethnicity, race, or religion; when we intend to dance the tango, our collective goal is to dance the tango; and so on. When we intend something collectively, there is an understanding that we, as a unity, intend to bring it about together. Some collective goals can only be brought about collectively; collectivity is inherent in our understanding of the nature of the action required to achieve them. In the foregoing list, only the goal of genocide is, potentially, not this kind of goal. Not only does international law include statutes according to which individuals may commit "acts of genocide" but also it is theoretically possible that one individual may successfully perpetrate a genocide—we can imagine cases in which a weapon of mass destruction could be deployed against a large target population or cases in which the group an individual intends to destroy has so few members that one person could conceivably destroy it.[18] In fact, it matters little to my account whether a collective goal is inherently collective or only incidentally so. The important feature of it is that the members embrace it as the collective's goal. In so doing, they understand their contributions in the context of the collective goal.

1.3.2 Can Individual Participants Intend Collective Actions?

The goal of a collective should not be understood strictly as something any individual member of the collective can intend. The proper subject of a collective intention with a collective goal as its object is a collective agent. Individuals' intentions oriented toward the collective's goal are to be understood as intentions to participate in collective action. Kutz captures this idea in his notion of participatory intentions, which he explains as intentions to participate in joint action.[19] Tuomela's notion of a we-intention is also, at bottom, the notion of an individual's intention to participate in joint action. He describes it as "in a non-literal sense—a participant's 'slice' of the joint intention, and an aim-intention based on a group reason."[20]

Tuomela draws a distinction between action-intentions and aim-intentions. If I have an action-intention about something, then I must think it possible for me to perform that action. Realistically, then, I can only have action-intentions about my own, individual actions—these might include contributions to collective actions, but they cannot include collective actions themselves. This condition on intention captures the intuition that what we intend must be, in some sense, under our control. I cannot, for example, intend to paint the sky blue. Where aim-intentions are concerned, agents do not have to believe they can bring about the aim by their actions alone; "rather the agent is assumed *by his actions to contribute* to the aimed result."[21] The distinction appears useful at first, since it acknowledges the intuition that the intentions of an individual are constrained by what it is possible for that individual to achieve through her actions—such intentions would be action-intentions. Adding the notion of an aim-intention is a bonus of sorts, since it allows individuals to intend (in some sense) actions and outcomes that are not in their hands alone; they require a collective effort. Where we-intentions are concerned, they are also informed and formed by the intentions of the collective (in Tuomela's technical vocabulary, these are joint intentions). But stipulating a second kind of intention—an aim-intention—is not sufficient to make it the case that individual agents, even those with we-intentions, can intend group aims. Tuomela's characterization of we-intentions as intentions to participate in joint action enables us to understand them as action-intentions with a limited scope, insofar as individuals are able to intend their contributions to collective actions. Bratman has suggested the use of the locution "I intend that we J," where "J" stands in for a joint action, in order to capture the intentional relationship between individual intention and a collective action.[22] The trick of course is to explain, whether in the case of an intention to or an intention that, how an individual can intend matters that are partly up to other people. On my view, the solution to this difficulty is simple: she or he cannot. Individuals can, however, intend their own part. This is not to say that collective actions cannot be intended at all. Collectives can intend collective actions: *we* can intend to make dinner together; *they* can intend to play street hockey. My view differs from those who would stop at intentions to participate because I maintain that there is a real sense in which collectives can and do intend to do what they do. I deny that a fully reductive account of collective intentions to the intentions of individuals can be given. We should not think of them as something that distributes neatly among individual members of collectives.

Nevertheless, in a goal-oriented collective, members' intentions play an important analytical role in the intentions of the whole. When we intend to do something together, then each of us individually has a commitment to the collective goal and an intention concerning his part of what we intend to do. The intention of each is not, however, a collective intention. It is an individual intention with collective content. These individual intentions with collective content are components of the collective intention. If, for example, we intend to take part in the wave, then each of us intends to take part, namely, when the wave gets to our section, each of us intends to jump up, throw our arms in the air, cheer, and then sit down. And we intend to do this in a coordinated fashion, based on our observations of when it is our turn. Our reason for doing this is to participate in the collective goal of producing a strong wave. If you were attending the game with me and I jumped up, threw my hands in the air, cheered, and then quickly sat down, you would have reason—in the absence of a wave or of the supposition that I was trying to get one started—to wonder what on earth I was doing. In the context of a wave, however, it is quite clear that I intend to participate in the collective action.

Another consideration in discussions of collective intention is the extent to which common knowledge of and/or mutual responsiveness to the intentions of other members is required. As the example just mentioned shows, the intentions of each in a coordinated, joint action respond to the intentions, or at least the perceived intentions, of the others. It is not enough simply for me to intend that we do the wave or even for me to intend to do my part in the wave. Rather, a good portion of those in the stands must also intend it and must be aware of and responsive to the intentions of those around them if the thing is going to happen at all.

Note that it is not the case that I cannot intend to embark on my part of a joint venture without your intending to do your part and without believing that our respective intentions will result in action. Clearly, we do not want to rule out that possibility. But in cases such as those, when my intention to participate in a collective action does not take into account the intentions of other participants in any way, then the conditions for collective intention have, arguably, not been met—at least by me. We may think of these conditions and the condition of common knowledge as being strongly or weakly met. Recognizing a continuum in this way allows space for degrees of collectivity. Not all collectives are equally cohesive. Some are "tighter" than others; this tightness will be reflected in the strength of the collective intention. With this idea in mind, I now consider the role of common knowledge in collective intention.

1.3.3 Common Knowledge

How much do participants need to know, or at a minimum reasonably believe, about the intentions, commitments, and expectations of other participants? I have already emphasized the importance of participants' sense of themselves as standing in relation to other members of the collective in the pursuit of a collective goal. This sense of oneself as a member of a group, standing in the relation of comember or coparticipant with other members of the group, is a significant factor in establishing conditions of collectivity as opposed to merely parallel action (even when such parallel action has a cumulative result). Conditions of common knowledge are frequently cited as a basis for collectivity. As Bratman points out, common knowledge provides some cognitive linkage between the participants—they are aware of the intentions of others as coparticipants in a joint venture. Accounts vary as to what the common knowledge must be knowledge of and as to how informed people must be. In Bratman's account, each knows of the others' intention "that we J," where J specifies a particular collective action. On other accounts, each must be aware of others' intentions to do their part to achieve the collective goal. Failures of awareness yield the result that individuals might be engaged in parallel, but not collective, action. Kutz offers a more minimalist account, arguing that the only requirement for collective action is that "the members of the group overlap in the conception of the collective end to which they intentionally contribute."[23] He offers a normative reason for the more minimalist account, pointing out that "ethically complex cases of joint action rarely involve perfect common knowledge, wholly shared conception of the joint act, or highly responsive strategic interactions."[24] I agree with Kutz that full common knowledge is too stringent a demand. I am not moved to this view by Kutz's examples, however, which are not, according to my view, examples of collective action. The first kind of example he offers is of an agent who, as Kutz describes, begins to do what will become part of a collective action if others follow his lead. This agent may have no expectations about others' participation. His action may go nowhere, or it may start something—either what he hopes to start or something entirely different. I maintain that actions of this sort are best described in terms of efforts to begin collective actions, not strictly parts of collective actions. Returning to my example of the wave, failed attempts to start waves at sports events abound. One or two people jump up and cheer, trying to get everyone else going, and no one joins them. Kutz's second example involves a spontaneous activity: two people saving a picnic from the rain. One person grabs the sandwiches and heads for the car, intending to do his part to save the picnic, and hoping that his friend will grab the drinks and the blanket. If the friend comes through, says Kutz, then it is reasonable to claim that they have jointly intentionally saved the picnic.[25] But actions taken independently of each other in this manner do not amount to jointly intentional action, even if they resulted in saving the picnic. As I have said, an agent's conception of herself or himself as standing in relation to others and working together toward a collective goal is an important feature of collective action. It would not even be enough if just one of the picnickers thought they were acting together. For example, one might mistakenly believe the other heard him shout "Grab the drinks and the blanket and run to the car." In order to get collectivity into the picture something slightly different needs to happen. There needs to be some mutual understanding—it could even be implicit, based on nothing more than one catching the other's eye and gesturing toward the drinks and the blanket. But if each party acts independently, then *they* do not act as a unit. Despite my thinking that Kutz's examples lack collectivity, I fully agree with him that requirements of common knowledge need to be more closely examined and ultimately relaxed.

In cases involving two persons, a common knowledge requirement is relatively easy to meet. If two of us intend to make dinner together, then it is easy for me to know how you understand yourself in relation to me and to our collective goal and to know that you intend to do your part. However, in a multiperson case it can be much more difficult. Consider a multilocation fundraiser involving thousands of participants across the country, such as "The Run for the Cure" and the many other fundraisers of this kind (the MS Bike Tour, the Parkinson's Walk, the Terry Fox Run). It is surely impossible that anyone knows all of the other participants or even who all of the other participants are. Does that mean that there is a failure of the common knowledge condition and that, therefore, no collective intention to fundraise and no collective action takes place? I believe that it would be a mistake to think of the common knowledge condition in this way. The difficulty is not the philosophical challenge that the conditions for knowledge are not going to met in the multi-person case; even the two-person case is not going to stand up to the strict knowledge requirements demanded by epistemologists. Rather, the issue turns on the scope and content of the common knowledge claim. What are the various participants required to know in terms of who else is involved and what their intentions are? If the goal of the common knowledge requirement is to provide enough cognitive linkage to secure collective, rather than parallel, action, then it ought to be enough to know, or at least have good grounds for believing, that others embrace the collective goal, see themselves in relation to other participants as members of a collective, and act with the intention of doing their part to raise money for cancer research. It is not the case that people need to know who all the relevant others are. The relevant beliefs about other participants admit of degrees, which in turn contribute to more or less cohesive-ness among groups and more or less jointness in their collective actions. In other words, some collective intentions are more collective than others. The strongest collective intentions will involve complete transparency. At the other extreme, where there is no mutual awareness of others involved, we simply have parallel activity. As I mentioned earlier, we might think of this feature of collectivity as "tightness." Some collectives and some intentional collective actions are more tightly collective than others.

1.3.4 Tightness and Degrees of Collectivity

Varied potential for common knowledge and the variance in degrees of collectivity along the dimensions of tightness that accompanies it do not only depend on the size of the collective. It can have also to do with the nature of the collective activity. The case in which you and I make dinner together tonight is a simple case involving full collectivity. If we intend to make dinner together tonight, we have the collective goal of making dinner together tonight. Having the collective goal means we approach the task as a unit and we understand ourselves as functioning in this unified manner. Moreover, each of us, respectively, has a self-understanding of her respective contribution and the nature of our subsequent interaction based on our commitment to that goal. In this case, I understand myself as making dinner with you, and you understand yourself as making dinner with me. We think of ourselves as standing in relation to each other as members of a group oriented toward the achievement of a particular collective goal. Our individual acts in the aid of that goal are guided by our sense of ourselves as a unit, as well as by the knowledge and expectations of each concerning the other's attitudes and intentions toward the goal. In this case, if we are to make dinner together successfully, then each of us needs each to know that that is what we, as a group, are intending. Each needs to be aware of the collective goal as a collective goal if the action toward its achievement is to be a collective action. Of course, we can intend it without it coming about—we might burn dinner and end up going to a restaurant or ordering in instead, or one of us might run into an emergency that requires we postpone our plan.

As described, this two-person example involves full collectivity—each participant in the collective act has the appropriate understanding of the quite specific collective goal, her respective contributions toward the goal, her intention as contributor to contribute, the intention of her coparticipant to do the same. Under these conditions, they pursue the goal as a unit. The combination of factors that brings about the collective activity is the state of affairs that constitutes the collective intention. It is out of these conditions that the collective's actions arise.

Consider a different case, that of a book group that meets monthly to discuss a book over a potluck dinner. Though some members are known to bring the same "genre" of food contribution each month—Joan will bring a rice dish, Kathleen can be counted on to bring a cake, Nancy most often makes a salad—the group makes no effort to coordinate the meal. The rest of the members are unpredictable. Sometimes, there is only salad. If Kathleen can't make it, there may be no dessert.

This dinner involves moderate collectivity. The lack of specificity of the goal and lack of knowledge about what others will do loosens the collectivity. Nevertheless, collective intention is not fully absent; the collective—that is, the book group—intends to have a potluck dinner. Whenever the group ends up with a good balance of hors d'oeuvres, salads, main courses, and desserts and when the respective dishes complement one another especially well, the members pat themselves on the back for a great team effort. But of course it isn't really a team effort; luck plays a major part in the outcome. The outcome is much more the satisfaction of a collective hope than the achievement of a collective goal. The group does not in any sense aim at or, as a group, intend, to produce a balanced meal of well-matched contributions.

Contrast this with a more coordinated potluck. This one is a themed event—the Vegetarian Indian Potluck (VIP). Everyone invited considers herself or himself to be contributing to a collective effort with a well-defined goal. The goal is to produce a meal that covers all the bases of a good vegetarian Indian meal. As a group, it is clear that this would not be achieved if everyone brought only samosas. They aim at the full range, from mango lassis and Indian beer, samosas and pakoras, to rice, dahl, paneer, korma, channa masala, a selection of breads and condiments, gulab jamun, and chai. If someone doesn't know what to bring, his contribution is governed by what is already on the table. If they have enough rice, but no naan, then he can supply the naan. Contributors must be guided by the collective intention. Those who stake out their claim early have more latitude as to what they may bring. The closer the group gets toward meeting its goal, the more constrained will be the options to contribute for the individual who intends to participate in the realization of the group's goal. As the evening progresses, they may truly compliment themselves for a job well done. The collective intention is satisfied, the collective goal is achieved. The level of coordination in the collective's activities toward the goal exhibits its tightness. This could be achieved with or without full common knowledge. There may be a sign-up sheet whereby each participant can see clearly what the others intend to bring. Or there may be a point person who has been delegated the task. The others know that the effort is being coordinated but may have only a partial awareness of which dishes have been spoken for and who is bringing what. Either way, it makes sense to say the action is fully collective, particularly in contrast with the true potluck described previously.

What do we gain by recognizing that collectivity comes in degrees? The greatest gain is that we have a concept of collectivity that reflects the reality of collective activity and a means of capturing a broad range of examples and articulating the differences between them with respect to their intentional character. On one end of the continuum is full collectivity and on the other end is parallel action. At and near the end where there is full collectivity, the combination of factors—much like the structures and mechanisms in organizations—produces a collective intention. No such intention arises in parallel action. The collective intention is neither a simple aggregate of individual intentions nor an individual intention with an irreducibly collective orientation. Rather, it is a state of affairs in which agents understand themselves as members of a collective and in relation to others, aiming as a group for the achievement of a collective goal, intend individually to do their part in the achievement of the collective goal, and mutually understand one another as doing the same. These conditions set the intention for the collective.

1.3.5 Bindingness

In her plural subject account of shared intention, Margaret Gilbert maintains that individuals come together to form a plural subject when they "intend as a body to pursue a joint goal."[26] Once the plural subject is formed and the shared intention established, two conditions take effect, captured in two criteria: the "criterion of obligation" and the "criterion of permission." The criterion of obligation stipulates that once the plural subject's intentions are established, individuals do not direct them. They become bound by its goals and subject to its intentions. Most theorists acknowledge that collective goals inform and shape the goals and intentions of individual participants. Gilbert is alone, however, in maintaining that the goals and intentions of the collectives bind participants by way of an obligation. This bindingness is further captured in the criterion of permission, according to which simply opting out is not an option: anyone wishing to be released from a collective intention must acquire the permission of other members.

In my view, once in effect, a collective intention may pose constraints on individuals' participation but should not be understood as obligating anyone to continue participating. Recall the vegetarian Indian potluck. In that example, the collective intention to have a nicely balanced vegetarian Indian meal has an organizing effect on the participants. It guides and constrains their contributions. To the extent that given individuals share the collective goal and think of themselves as members of the group standing in relation to others committed to the same goal, they will allow their contributions to be shaped by that goal. This is not to say, however, that they cannot opt out. One individual's opting out will not, in a multiperson example, be enough to eliminate the collective intention. It may increase the chances of its not being satisfied—if, for example, the person opting out was in charge of the naan, the meal will be incomplete in that respect and the collective's goal will not be fully met. When there are only two people in a given collective, for example when we intend to make dinner together, one person's withdrawing from the plan is enough to eliminate the collective intention. That it will end the collective intentional action is not a good reason to forbid it or to require that permission need be given. It may be rude to back out of plans made and impolite to dash another's reasonable expectations, but the risk of bad manners is not a strong basis for an obligation. For this reason I believe that while a collective intention may influence, shape, and even constrain the nature of an individual's contribution to a collective action, there is nothing built into the notion of a collective intention that makes it obligate.

1.3.6 The Collectivist Character of the View

The view I have outlined here is more collectivist than individualist. I believe that its collectivist character is a great asset. The collectivism is based in the notion that the collective intention and action operate at a different level from individual intention and action. Much like a supervenience theory of the mind in which mental phenomena are based in but not identical with or reducible to material or physical phenomena, I argue that collective intentions and actions are dependent on, even based in, but by no means identical with or reducible to individual intentions and actions. Indeed, the levels interact with each other, and the interaction may go both ways. Furthermore, the existence of a distinct collective level of intention, even if it depends on features of the individual level, supports the idea of collective agency. The structural features of goal-oriented collectives in action give rise to intentional actions that cannot be understood as the actions of individuals. My earlier remarks about organic unities help to lend substance to this view. An organic unity admittedly has parts, but the whole is a unity to which a simple summation of its parts cannot do justice. In addition, my discussion of the examples of making dinner together and of the two potlucks demonstrate that collectivity comes in degrees. More collectivity supports a more intentional sense of collective purpose. In cases such as those (e.g., the vegetarian Indian potluck), individual contributions are more constrained by the goals and intentions of the collective than in cases where there is less collectivity.

The analysis provided here of the collective intentional structure of goal-oriented collectives leaves room for a robust discussion of individual responsibility in these collective action scenarios without dismissing the idea that there is a distinct level of collective responsibility about which we may also legitimately speak.

1.4 CONCLUSION

The goal of this chapter has been to articulate the difference in intentional structure between two kinds of collective agents: organizations and goal-oriented collectives. The accounts are meant to establish that there is a plausible story to be told about agency at the collective level in the cases of organizations and of goal-oriented collectives. The notion of collective agency has great normative merit. In particular, as I argue in the next chapter, it enables us to account for collective moral responsibility.

[2]

COLLECTIVE MORAL RESPONSIBILITY

Just as there is an individualist and collective notion of collective action, where the individualists think of it as a reductive concept and the collectivists think of it more holistically, so there is an individualist and collective notion of collective moral responsibility. In the previous chapter, I distinguished between two kinds of collectives capable of intentional action—organizations and goal-oriented collectives. I gave an account of their respective intentional structures as a means of giving substance to the claim that collectives' intentional actions flow from their intentions. The normative picture that follows from this account is quite simple. If, as I have claimed, we may understand collective action as operating at a different level from individual action, then we may understand collective moral responsibility as different from individual responsibility and as being justified by appeal to collective intentions and the actions to which they give rise. Collective moral responsibility is not, therefore, a function of the moral responsibility of individuals. Instead, it is a function of the agency of collectives. The goal of this chapter is to explain, motivate, and defend my account of collective moral responsibility. I begin with my understanding of what collective moral responsibility is.

2.1 WHAT IS COLLECTIVE MORAL RESPONSIBILITY?

Moral responsibility is the blameworthiness or praiseworthiness that we attribute to agents for their actions. Agents warrant praise when they do the right thing, blame when they do the wrong thing. Collective moral responsibility is the blameworthiness and praiseworthiness of collectives for their actions. No differently from human moral agents, collectives warrant praise when they do the right thing, blame when they do the wrong thing. The responsibility of collectives is not the blameworthiness and praiseworthiness of their members, though collectives' responsibility does not rule out that some or even all of the members might be blameworthy or praiseworthy for the part they play in collective action. This view of collective moral responsibility requires that collectives be agents capable of intentional action. Chapter 1 explained how we ought to understand the intentions and actions of collectives; their actions can and should be understood in a way that distinguishes them from the actions of their members and from mere events, such as hurricanes and earthquakes. They are distinctive, insofar as they operate at a different level. Collectives exhibit agency because they are capable of intentional action.

The first reason, therefore, that we should take seriously the idea of collective moral responsibility is that organizations and goal-oriented collectives have intentional structures that legitimate the attribution of moral agency to them. These intentional structures do not require that collectives possess minds, brains, or heads in which to form their intentions. They do require us to acknowledge that, for all their dependency on individual agents, the intentions and actions of collectives are different from those of their members.

In what follows, I offer two additional reasons to take the idea of collective moral responsibility seriously. The first reason is action-theoretic; the second is a normative implication of the first.

2.2 WHY WE NEED COLLECTIVE MORAL RESPONSIBILITY

Collective agents, not their members, are the agents who perform collective actions. Therefore, collective moral responsibility is needed in order to account for moral responsibility for collective actions. In what follows, I expand on this point.

Earlier, I talked about different kinds of collective actions. Some actions have an inherent collectivity, insofar as they can only be performed collectively. These would include playing a symphony, getting married, and doing the wave at a sports event. They require, respectively, an orchestra, a couple, and a crowd in an arena or stadium. Other collective actions are in fact but not necessarily collective. Some people argue that genocide is like this because, hypothetically, one person could carry out a genocide.[1] By the same token, moving a grand piano might be this kind of act—it is generally a collective endeavor because average or even above average human strength is not up to the task. But we can imagine a hypothetical case in which someone has superhuman strength that enables her or him to lift a grand piano. In addition, a range of everyday activities, such as going for a walk, making dinner, or working in the garden might seem to fall under the category of actions that individuals can perform alone or together with others. My own view is that, for any action x, *doing x together* is an inherently collective act. I spend no time defending that view because, in the end, I do not think there is an important distinction between inherently and only incidentally collective acts. When performed, a collective act is the act of a collective whether it is so necessarily or not. For that reason, I do not draw a sharp theoretical line between these categories of collective action. What does matter is that, whether inherently collective or not, some actions are performed by collectives, not by single individuals. Of these acts, at least some of them have moral dimensions and may be evaluated—even ought to be evaluated—in moral terms as right or wrong. To this extent, they are objects of moral responsibility and the agents who perform them may be blameworthy or praiseworthy. In the case of collective actions, it is collective agents who are blameworthy or praiseworthy. The individuals who contribute to the outcome do not—actually cannot—perform or intend the whole act even if they may share the collective goal and contribute to its achievement. The collective intends and performs the action. Therefore, in relation to the act as a whole—that is, in relation to the collective act—only the collective as such is morally responsible.

Consider an example. Every year, across Canada, thousands of people participate in the Terry Fox Run to raise millions of dollars for cancer research. In a typical year, the Run generates over $20 million. No one individual raises that amount, but the collective does and, in fact, intends to raise as much as possible. To the extent that no individual raises the whole amount, no individual is fully responsible for it—that is, no one is praiseworthy for raising $20 million. Yet fundraising $20 million is surely a praiseworthy achievement, the moral magnitude of which is not captured in any one contribution, which is the only other place agency might lie. I am not here concerned to say anything about the moral responsibility of individuals for their contributions. Individual responsibility in cases of collective action will be the subject of a later chapter.[2] Here, I want only to establish a claim that is the simple normative counterpart of my claim that collective intentional action takes place at a different level from individual actions. Normatively speaking, the different levels of intentional action support different levels of moral responsibility. Attending only to the level of individual action would constitute a loss and leave us incapable of drawing conclusions about moral responsibility at the collective level, sometimes in cases of extreme moral significance. Let me say more about this claim, for not everyone will countenance the view that failing to address responsibility at the collective level constitutes a loss.

Some theorists might claim, for example, that collective acts are merely aggregates of members' contributions. If this is right, there is no reason to feel pressed to account for responsibility of the whole because the contributions are fully accounted for at the individual level. This argument would suggest that our normative discussion can remain at the level of the individual without any normative loss to the assessment of responsibility. The lingering question is whether they are correct in this conclusion. I offer three reasons for thinking they are incorrect and that there would indeed be a normative loss. First, it is a metaphysical fact that the collectives in question perform as agents, and for this reason they count as responsible. With respect to this reason, the normative loss amounts to a failure to account for a normative reality: the moral responsibility of a certain type of moral agent, namely, collective moral agents. If these agents are, as I have aimed to show, morally responsible, then we have reason to evaluate them as such. But this point might be thought to sidestep the real issue. According to some, the real issue is that countenancing the collective level of responsibility does not add anything worthwhile to our normative analysis. If we can satisfactorily account for the responsibility of individuals, then we should be content to rest there. The two further reasons address this response. Second, as outlined above, if the individuals and the collective perform different acts, and if the individuals' acts and the collective's acts are both morally significant, then the collective act is not adequately accounted for by individual assessments of moral responsibility. Returning to the example above, raising $20 million for charity is a moral act of a different magnitude from contributing $200.

Finally, the third response to the objection that there is no normative loss invites us to think more carefully about the way individual acts in collective contexts come by their moral features. An individual's participation in running a race would have no moral quality in the absence of the fundraising context or some similarly morally compelling circumstance. That is to say, the act derives its morally salient features from the fundraising context itself. We might admire people who complete the Boston Marathon, but their race lacks the moral features of those participating in the Terry Fox Run or the Run for the Cure. Taking part in a massive coordinated effort to raise money for a worthy cause adds a moral dimension to an act that might otherwise have none. The participants' acts have the additional feature of being "a part of that," where "that" is an undeniably praiseworthy collective effort. In these cases, we cannot fully capture the moral significance of individuals' actions until we see them in the context of the collective action and its significance. Morally speaking, the collective act—whether inherently or incidentally collective—is more fundamental than the acts of the individuals, insofar as the moral weight of the collective act defines the moral dimensions of the acts of individuals. The claim being made here is that in moral terms, individuals' contributions to collective acts inherit relevant moral features from the collective action context in which they occur, not the other way around. Thus, the moral assessment of the collective level of action as blameworthy or praiseworthy gives rise to the normative evaluation of individual contributions.

Let us look at one more example, that of genocide. If there is a commonsense understanding of genocide, it would be its characterization as a large-scale atrocity with many victims and involving a great many perpetrators. That is, a successful, nearly successful, or even realistically attempted genocide is perpetrated against a group and carried out by organizations or goal-oriented collectives. Given this understanding of genocide, an individual does not fully perpetrate a genocide even if he contributes to it. We find the only exceptions in dreamt-up cases in which the mere push of a button would wipe out the target group or in which the relevant group has only a handful of members. In this "ordinary" concept of genocide, we imagine it as a mass atrocity committed by a number of perpetrators over a period of time.[3] We can point to particular genocides, for example, the Holocaust and the Rwandan genocide, which constitute collective atrocities whose moral magnitude is simply not captured by isolating the contributions, no matter how great, of any one participant. Rather, in much the same way that raising $20 million is of a different moral order from contributing $200, perpetrating a genocide involving millions of victims is of a different moral order from a lesser contribution performed in the context of the whole. Genocide—that is, the destruction of an entire group—is the collective goal toward which the collective aims. As argued above, the act of the individual, intentionally performed as a contribution to the particular whole, derives its moral significance and morally relevant description—for example, "contribution to genocide"—from its intentional performance.

I have now provided examples of praiseworthy and blameworthy collective actions and argued that we cannot appreciate the moral magnitude of the collective acts without a normative view at the collective level. In sum, I believe that an overly individualistic account of collective agency does not take the collective view seriously enough. It sidesteps the fact of collective agency, it inadequately captures moral responsibility for collective actions as such—actions whose moral magnitude is frequently of a different order from that of the individual acts that contribute to them—and it does not allow a satisfactory explanation of the way individual acts in morally significant collective action contexts acquire their moral qualities. The best way to address these concerns, I maintain, is to uphold the distinction between the individual level and the collective level of moral responsibility.

2.3 OBJECTIONS AND REPLIES

There are a number of objections to the idea of collective moral responsibility that require attention before moving on. They are worth considering at some length because they capture a widespread tendency among philosophers and nonphilosophers alike to gravitate toward individualism. In what follows, I consider six individualist worries about collective moral responsibility and argue that, given an adequate understanding of collective moral responsibility, all six are unfounded. The concerns I take up in what follows are:

1. Collective moral responsibility holds some people responsible for the actions of others
2. Collective moral responsibility punishes innocent individuals
3. Collective moral responsibility precludes individual moral responsibility in collective action situations
4. Collective moral responsibility reifies social structures and other abstract entities

5. Collective moral responsibility requires collective intentions, but collectives cannot have intentions because intentions are mental states, and collectives lack consciousness

6. There is no *interesting* sense of collective moral responsibility

I begin with the objection that collective moral responsibility holds some people responsible for the actions of others. Of all the challenges to collective moral responsibility, this one is perhaps the most frequently cited. Any plausible account of collective moral responsibility will not hold some people responsible for the actions of others. It would be disingenuous to stop there, however; the concerns underpinning the worry are legitimate and worth considering. Holding people responsible for acts for which they are not responsible would be an unfair mistake. H. D. Lewis considers the idea of collective moral responsibility to be "barbarous" because he believes that if a collective is responsible, then all of its members must also be responsible.[4] He assumes that collective moral responsibility automatically distributes among the responsible collective's members. He finds this consequence to be objectionable because it may be the case that not all members of a blameworthy collective participated in the blameworthy wrongdoing. Lewis is entirely correct to claim that there is no necessary connection between being a member of a blameworthy collective and having participated in the wrongdoing. In some cases, many may be innocent. Note, however, that collective moral responsibility need not be understood in a distributive way. While a determination of collective moral responsibility might well give us reason to examine the contributions of individuals and evaluate their responsibility for their parts, it is not the case that individuals are blameworthy as individuals for collective actions. I advocate a more nuanced view that emphasizes the importance of distinguishing questions of collective moral responsibility from questions of individual moral responsibility in cases of collective action. If the responsibility of collectives is distinct from the responsibility of individuals, then any claim that we make about the responsibility of collectives will not automatically have implications for individuals. Once we recognize the distinction between these two levels, then if blame does turn out to be laid on the innocent, that would be a mistake. It does not follow from a collective's being morally responsible that any given member played a part. This is especially true with respect to organizations, where people in different roles are differently engaged with the actions of the organization and have different capacities to direct those actions. How to implicate individuals in collective action situations and for what to consider them responsible are questions at a distinct level of normative inquiry. Individualists who worry that collective moral responsibility requires holding some people responsible for the actions of others do not recognize that a collective can be responsible without all of its members being responsible.

At this point, the individualist would be perfectly reasonable to ask about the relationship between a morally responsible collective and its members. Does being a member of a collective that is, for example, blameworthy have no normative implications at the individual level? Most of us have a strong intuition that when a collective is responsible at least some of its members are also responsible. The intuition stems from our understanding of collective action as involving the acts of individuals. As outlined in the previous chapter, we have every reason to think the actions of individuals contribute to and are in large part constitutive of the acts of collectives. Respecting the intuition does not, however, require a distributive understanding of collective action. We may observe two notable points. First, even on a two-level view of moral responsibility, it makes sense to think that where a collective is responsible at least some of its members are. Some of them intentionally contribute to the collective's act and share in the collective's goal. Second, an often overlooked fact is that the collective and its members are not responsible for the same act. Whereas a collective is responsible for the collective act, individual members are responsible for their contributions, and the degree of their responsibility will depend, in part, on the extent to which they share in the collective's goals and act with a view to participating in bringing those goals about. Members of goal-oriented collectives, therefore, are much more likely to be morally implicated in collective wrongdoing because, in at least some of these cases, a commitment to the collective goal and action together with others to achieve that goal is a fundamental part of what it means to be a member of the collective at all. This does not hold true for membership in organizations, particularly in large organizations and particularly for people occupying lower level roles in the organizational hierarchy. None of these observations undermines the claim that simply being a member of a morally responsible collective does not automatically implicate a person in what that collective does even if it might give us reasons to subject the person's actions to close moral scrutiny. The preceding discussion responds to the objection that collective moral responsibility holds innocent individuals responsible for the deeds of others.

Sometimes the concern about condemning the innocent focuses on the second of the six worries, namely, that collective moral responsibility requires that innocent individuals be *punished* for collective wrongs. If one consequence of establishing an agent as blameworthy is that a just response should involve punishment as a form of desert, one might worry that it is not possible to punish a collective without punishing its members.[5] If a collective entity such as a nation or a corporation is punished, there may be negative effects on the innocent as well as on the guilty members of the collective.

Consider a case in which a large insurance company is fined for corrupt practices. The fines are so enormous that the company cannot pay them without closing down some of its operations. These closures have an impact on some of the corrupt, but they also result in job losses for people who had no hand in the corrupt practices and loss of stock value for the shareholders. Thus, it is claimed, punishing the corporation is tantamount to punishing innocent members of the corporation. Similarly, people have claimed that in cases involving government reparations for past wrongs, taxpayers—many or even all of whom were not alive when the wrongs were committed—end up bearing the cost of the punishment. A conceptual point bears making here, and that is that even when individual human agents are punished, their punishment sometimes has a negative impact on innocent others. But it would be wrong to think of all suffering as a form of punishment. If we think of punishment as a retributive response to a transgression, thereby meted out to the guilty party as a matter of desert, it would be a category mistake to claim that the innocent who suffer when we punish the guilty are *punished* for the crimes of the guilty. Think about the case of an individual murderer whose family may suffer if the murderer is punished. That the family members suffer does not mean they are being punished for someone else's crime or that it is unjust to punish the murderer. But perhaps the conceptual response is insufficient or at least unsatisfying because somewhat cavalier. The objection, some might insist, runs deeper. What is objectionable is that where collective punishment is concerned, the costs are *always* going to be borne by innocent members and the collective as such will feel nothing. There is just no getting around it. As the famous line about corporations goes: they have "no souls to damn and no bodies to kick."[6] The implication is that a collective entity of this kind cannot be hurt, so, assuming punishment is meant to inflict pain, any punishment or threat of punishment will be ineffective against its intended recipient. I take the discussion of adequate responses to evaluations of blameworthy collective behavior seriously. We need to recognize that collective wrongdoing, in the same ways as individual wrongdoing, may warrant a variety of responses; these may or may not include punishment. There is no necessary connection between determining that collectives are morally responsible and requiring that those found blameworthy must be punished. It may be the case that alternative forms of response are necessary.[7] Few people think that wrongdoing, whether individual or collective, should have no consequences at all. The challenge is to determine how to respond to attributions of blameworthy collective moral responsibility. This will require a discussion of the function of punishment—is the function expressive, deterrent, retributive, rehabilitative? It will also require understanding whether and what forms of punishment will be effective or whether we should prefer alternatives to punishment. Given that punishment may or may not be the best way of dealing with collective wrongdoing and given that, if it is, we must consider appropriate forms of collective punishment that minimize the impact on innocent members, it is not clear that the suffering of innocents is a necessary implication of determinations of blameworthy collective moral responsibility. Moreover, much as it makes sense to minimize the suffering of innocents, it bears repeating that the suffering of innocents as a result of either individual or collective punishment does not, itself, constitute the punishment of innocents.

The third individualist worry is that if collective moral responsibility does not condemn every member of the collective, then it precludes us from attributing responsibility to any individuals at all. This concern stems from the claim that, given that collective moral responsibility is not reducible to or explained in terms of individual moral responsibility, anything that we say about the blameworthiness of collectives falls short when it comes to individual responsibility. Jan Narveson maintains that "that is what is wrong with collective responsibility. Precisely because it will not reduce, it precludes you from getting at anybody—all you can do is wave flags and write poems."[8] But it is not the case that all you can do is wave flags and write poems; collective responsibility does not exhaust the possibilities for assigning responsibility in these cases. There is no reason to think that the collective level of responsibility precludes the possibility of responsibility-attributions at the level of individuals. Earlier I argued that analyzing the actions of individuals as contributions to a larger collective act with moral dimensions is the best way to capture the particular moral features of these individual contributions. It is not the case that collective responsibility is the only responsibility there is in cases of collective action. Thus, there is no reason to think that individual responsibility must fall by the wayside where there is collective moral responsibility.

The fourth individualist reason for rejecting collective responsibility is related to the third concern that it does not allow us to "get at" individuals. According to this fourth worry, collective moral responsibility holds "social structures" or "society in general" responsible for the crimes of the less fortunate. Making reference to a case in which a woman steals bread to feed her starving children, Lewis says that social structures and society in general

> are both abstractions which we must be careful not to hypostatize. What should be said, if we are to speak exactly, is this. The guilt of the poor woman is lessened, if not eliminated altogether, by her circumstances. But she alone is to blame, if blame there is to be, for what she herself has done. Others are also to blame, but for something else, namely for their part in allowing her to remain in desperate need. But they are responsible for this as

individuals, and strictly in proportion to what each might have done, directly or indirectly, to ameliorate her lot.[9]

I want to focus on the worry about reifying abstract entities. The first notable point is that Lewis provides no argument; he simply warns the reader to be careful not to do so. Moreover, this analysis makes no room for systemic injustices or for collective actions. In the case under discussion, there may be no direct or even indirect wrongdoing that is traceable to the "others [who] are also to blame." It is not just logistically challenging to apportion blame among individuals in cases of widespread wrongful social practice; in some cases individuals are not to blame, and understanding the nature of their excusable wrongdoing requires making a moral comment about the nature of a society or culture as a whole.[10] Finally, it is not the case that agents of collective moral responsibility are typically considered to be "social structures" or "society in general." Organizations, as I have defined them, are highly structured collectives with identities that are independent of their members, and they are not as difficult to identify and define as social forces or social structures. And goal-oriented collectives exhibit more agency than the loosely conceived notion of society or social groups presupposed by the objection. Once we distinguish between types of collectives, we leave it an open question whether all types qualify as collective agents. I argue that not all do. If social groups count as collectives—and there exists a range of opinion on that question—it does not automatically follow that they are collective agents. Thus the worry that collective moral responsibility invokes the idea of social forces or social groups as moral agents, thereby reifying them in an ontologically unwelcome manner, misconstrues the reach of collective agency.

Sometimes the concern about reification of abstract entities is related to the fifth objection to collective moral responsibility, which assumes that it requires consciousness at the collective level. This concern rides piggyback on the widely held assumption that collective moral responsibility requires collective intentions, and that intentions are mental states.[11] But it is not the case that collective intentions require consciousness. In the previous chapter, I outlined a view according to which neither the intentions of organizations nor those of goal-oriented collectives require consciousness. Thus, though some accounts of collective intention may understand them as mental states that need to be housed in a collective mind, collective intentions do not need to be thought of in this way. As a result, the existence of collective agents capable of intentional action does not require that they be conscious entities with mental states.

The final objection from individualists is that there is no *interesting* sense of collective moral responsibility. I take this to mean that there is no sense of moral responsibility at the collective level that doesn't just reduce to moral responsibility at the level of individuals. Proponents of this view believe that ultimately, all moral responsibility is individual moral responsibility. Narveson claims, for example, that "underlying individualism is the only rational meta-theory for collective responsibility."[12] According to his view, "when groups are said to be responsible for this or that, the implication has to be that we may blame (or praise) members of the group, insofar as they are members, for the action(s) in question."[13] And finally, he asks, "is it in any interesting way true that responsibility for either [the Rwandan genocide or the Holocaust] is irreducibly collective? Is it true that the act in question is collective in that [irreducible] sense? No. Genocide involves thousands or millions of individual murders. The fact that all of the victims belonged to one group, G, and all the killers to another, F, does not mean that genocide is irreducible."[14] Recall the suggestion I made earlier that we have a commonsense distinction between the collective atrocity of genocide and contributions to genocide or acts of genocide at the individual level. Individuals do not perform the collective act even if their actions contribute to it. Moreover, actions for which collectives are responsible flow from collective intentions. The intentions of individuals are components of collective intentions, but collective intentions are more than just the sum total of individual intentions. Similarly, genocide is not simply the sum total of individual murders because the collective act of genocide is different in character from the murders or individual acts of genocide committed by individuals in the service of the collective goal. What makes it irreducible is that the relations between the intentions of individuals, their respective commitment to the collective goal, and their understanding of themselves as acting together with others who share the goal in order to bring the goal about are essential features of collective intentions. Aggregating individual intentions does not take seriously the interrelations between the intentions of individuals. Indeed, I argued in the previous chapter that individuals are unable to intend to perform collective actions. In addition, I argue that analyzing the actions of individuals as contributions to a larger, collective act with moral dimensions is the best way to capture the particular moral features of these individual contributions. Instead of claiming that in the absence of individual contributions there is no genocide, I highlight the point that in the absence of the context of genocide the individual contributions do not have the moral character that they do. Only an account of the moral features of collective action that takes this level of action seriously and requires that it be understood in intentional terms will provide the relevant conceptual underpinning for accurate assessments of individual moral responsibility in collective action contexts.

Individualists may ask again at this point whether this is an interesting sense of collective moral responsibility, wondering whether it is useful or needed. Can we do more with it than "wave flags and write poems?" I argue earlier in this chapter that without an account of what is wrong with, for example, genocide as a collective act, or what is morally good about raising $20 million for charity, we cannot adequately account for the respective blameworthiness and praiseworthiness of individual contributions. If this is the case, then the collectivist analysis of collective moral responsibility that I advocate in my two-level theory is useful and necessary if we want to retain individual moral responsibility in collective actions. I do not claim that individual murders or individual acts understood by international law to be acts of genocide are not wrong. Instead, we should say that when they are parts of a collective act of genocide their wrongness is of a distinct kind. They have the additional moral feature of being contributions to genocide. If the collective context provides an essential framework for an adequate normative analysis of individual contributions, then it is false that there is nothing interesting about the account of collective moral responsibility outlined here.

2.4 CONCLUSION

The discussion of these individualist objections helps to highlight the conceptual difficulties that arise when we inadequately appreciate the distinction between the collective and individual levels of moral responsibility, or when we believe that the collective level does no work.

I have argued that collective moral responsibility is a significant level of moral responsibility and that doing away with it in favor of a thoroughly individualistic approach to moral responsibility is too costly. My case for this view turns on two main points. First, collective acts with moral dimensions require analysis at the collective level because, as collective acts, they are not or cannot be performed by individuals. I deny that there is a theoretically significant distinction between acts that are inherently collective and those that are performable by individuals but, in a particular instance, are performed collectively. Second, in order to account for the moral significance of individual participation in collective action situations, it is necessary first to understand the moral nature of the collective action of which it is a part. I have also argued that recognizing collective moral responsibility as a distinct level of moral responsibility does not commit us to holding individuals responsible for the acts of others or to condemning and punishing the innocent. Furthermore, it does not commit us to claiming that collectives are conscious beings with mental states. Thus, in addition to developing a positive argument for the moral significance of the concept of collective responsibility, I have also addressed a number of reasons opponents of the concept have given in support of the view that individual moral responsibility is the only moral responsibility that there is.

In the next chapter, I turn to the notion of collective guilt. Much confusion surrounds the concept of collective guilt. My aim in the next chapter is to offer an understanding of collective guilt that distinguishes it from other kinds of guilt and from collective guilt feelings.

[3]

COLLECTIVE GUILT

In the previous chapters I outlined my view of collective moral responsibility, according to which collectives are morally responsible
agents capable of intentional action. If collectives are the sorts of
things that can be morally responsible, then there is a sense in which
they can be guilty, too. The threefold purpose of this chapter is to
provide an account of collective guilt as blameworthy collective
moral responsibility, to clarify some misconceptions about what
collective guilt might be, and to consider whether collective guilt
requires that we account for collective guilt feelings.

"Guilt" is an ambiguous term, so let me begin by stating that I
understand guilt as blameworthy moral responsibility. An agent is
guilty when she or he is morally responsible in the blameworthy
sense. Collective guilt, then, is blameworthy moral responsibility at
the collective level. Collectives with the capacity for intentional action are guilty whenever they are blameworthy for their actions. It is
important to distinguish collective guilt from individual or personal
guilt and from membership guilt. Even more fundamentally, it is
important to distinguish an agent's being guilty—an objective evaluation of moral responsibility—from an agent's believing herself to be
guilty and from an agent's feeling guilty. In ordinary language, when
we speak of "guilt" we frequently have in mind a moral emotion of

sorts. We think of guilt as something that we feel or experience when we believe ourselves to be in the wrong. But this sense of guilt is quite different from the normative concept that is the focus of this chapter, and, as I argue, thinking of guilt solely in terms of the experience of guilt creates confusion in discussions of collective guilt. I begin with a discussion of the difference between being guilty, believing oneself to be guilty, and feeling guilty.

3.1 GUILT: BEING, BELIEVING, AND FEELING

Let us start with the individual case. Few would dispute that I may be guilty, that is, be blameworthy for a wrong action that I have taken, without feeling guilty. A number of different circumstances could account for the discrepancy. For one, I may not recognize my wrongdoing; agents sometimes act wrongly while believing themselves to be in the right. In such cases, agents will not feel guilty. Guilt feelings require, at a minimum, a self-assessment of moral wrongdoing; they require that I believe myself to be guilty. It is also conceivable that I might believe myself to be guilty without experiencing any particular or distinctive feelings of guilt (however we may choose to characterize such feelings).[1] Alternatively, I may experience feelings of guilt while not being guilty in the objective sense. This situation arises when my self-assessment of moral wrongdoing is mistaken, that is, if I believe myself to be guilty when I am not guilty. With respect to individuals, then, there are three distinct conditions of guilt. The first, *being guilty*, is an objective moral condition—someone is guilty when she is morally responsible in the blameworthy sense for doing something wrong. The second, *believing oneself to be guilty*, involves a self-assessment that may or may not be consistent with the objective moral condition. The third, *experiencing feelings of guilt*, is an affective response to one's belief that one is guilty. Two points worth noting about feelings of guilt are, first, that they are not a necessary response to the belief that one is guilty, and second, that they are unfounded when the belief on which they are based is false.

Having noted three distinct conditions of guilt in the individual case, we can now turn to the collective case to see which of the three, if any, have collective counterparts. To the extent that at least some collectives are responsible agents capable of intentional collective action, at least some collectives may be guilty in the objective sense. Collective guilt in this sense is the same thing as blameworthy collective moral responsibility. I have given extensive attention to the reasons in favor of collective moral responsibility already, as well as provided an account of collective intention that supports the substantive notion of collective moral responsibility that I advocate. Given the attention to collective moral responsibility in earlier chapters, my focus here will not be on developing the account of objective collective guilt. Instead, as far as that sense of guilt is concerned, I shall argue that in the collective case, it is the most important of the three conditions of guilt outlined above. If collective belief is possible, then it is possible for collectives to have beliefs about their guilt. The government of Canada, for example, can believe that it is guilty for both its historical and present treatment of First Nations people, particularly where federal government policy has been and is concerned. With respect to *collective guilt feelings*, it is not clear that collectives are capable of affective responses at the collective level or that collective feelings play any necessary normative or practical role in collective guilt. I consider collective guilt feelings later in this chapter. For now, note that since feelings of guilt are distinct from the objective moral condition of guilt and from the belief in one's guilt, an adequate account of collective guilt does not require that we account for collective guilt feelings. In the following section, I distinguish between collective guilt, personal guilt, and membership guilt.

3.2 TYPES OF GUILT

Personal guilt is blameworthy moral responsibility at the individual level for one's own actions. There is a strong intuition that agents can be personally guilty only for what they, personally, have done. I cannot be personally guilty for the blameworthy actions of others because their actions are not mine. Collective guilt is blameworthy responsibility at the level of collectives. If a corporation exploits its workers, then the corporation is morally responsible, as a corporation, for exploiting its workers. It is blameworthy for that action, understood as a collective action. Its blameworthiness is a moral condition of the collective, not a moral condition of the individual members of the collective. It is in no way a species of personal guilt. Therefore, collective guilt and personal guilt are different because they operate at different levels. Given that personal guilt and collective guilt address guilt at different levels of agency and moral responsibility—the individual and the collective, respectively—an ascription of guilt to a collective does not have direct implications for the personal guilt of the members of the collective. Nevertheless, it is worth emphasizing that the lack of direct implications for personal guilt does not automatically rule out individual involvement and individual moral responsibility in the relevant collective action. Individuals may and do participate in and contribute to collective wrongdoing. However, these contributions do not render individuals responsible, as individuals, for collective action. How to understand individual moral responsibility in collective action contexts will be a subject taken up in subsequent chapters.

Since individuals do not perform collective actions, individuals cannot be personally guilty for the actions of collectives to which they belong. Another form of guilt from which we need to distinguish collective guilt is membership guilt. Membership guilt is difficult to define and difficult to make sense of. At the same time, people often have membership guilt in mind when they speak of collective guilt. To think of membership guilt as collective guilt is a mistake, because membership guilt is not a feature of the collective; it operates at an altogether different level. Thus, it is not collective guilt. Instead, membership guilt is a feature of individuals who are members of blameworthy collectives, regardless of whether they participate in the collective action for which their group is blameworthy. Those who are guilty in the membership sense are not guilty for the acts of the collective, but for their own acts or omissions in response to the collective action. Though the collective context is relevant for membership guilt, the guilt itself is not collective. In what follows, I argue that membership guilt is a species of personal guilt. I begin with an explanation of the difference between membership guilt and membership guilt feelings.

In addition to its being conflated with collective guilt, membership guilt is often run together with the idea of membership guilt feelings, which, it is claimed, amount to feelings of guilt experienced by an individual because of her or his association with others who have acted wrongly. If, for example, my team behaves in a deplorable way, then I might experience feelings of guilt even if I was on the sidelines and even if I could not stop them. But besides membership guilt feelings, there is also the phenomenon of membership guilt that is sometimes regarded as a kind of moral taint. The idea is that my association with people who act badly, including comembers of a group to which I belong, taints me in a manner that makes me share in their guilt. Here again we have an objective conception of guilt—I may be tainted without believing myself to be and, conversely, I may mistakenly believe myself to be tainted. Sometimes membership guilt is characterized as metaphysical, as opposed to moral, guilt.[2] Karl Jaspers characterizes the difference between moral guilt and metaphysical guilt by noting that the former, but not the latter, has its source in the blameworthy actions of the party who is in the relevant sense guilty. Those who are guilty in the metaphysical sense are so because of who they are, or more precisely, who they choose to be. In his discussion of membership guilt, Larry May notes that being members of a blameworthy collective is not in itself the violation of a moral duty. Nevertheless, he points out, how we position ourselves with respect to that group and its actions, the extent to which we enjoy a feeling of solidarity with the offending group, is a morally charged issue with consequences for one's moral character. There are actions we can take that "break the chain of responsibility" even if we cannot leave the relevant group. May notes, rightly, that not taking these actions amounts to choosing to identify with the group. Omissions of this kind constitute choices about who we consider ourselves to be. I agree that these choices send a message about who we think we are. In addition, they involve moral choices about our actions, not just existential choices about our identities. To that extent, they may also be the basis of moral guilt of individuals.

The distinction between metaphysical and moral guilt is useful because there do seem to be circumstances, particularly those into which we are born, in which people's continued compliance with the status quo speaks volumes about who they choose to be. When the status quo involves participation in wrongful social practice, the choice to live as a member of the group who participates, or even benefits from, this identity—for example, the German identity in Nazi Germany—the existential choice is metaphysical. One does not necessarily have to be a direct participant in wrongdoing to be guilty in this sense. Thus, metaphysical guilt allows us to cast a wider net of guilt over a population than moral guilt might (and certainly than criminal guilt for specifically proscribed crimes). Jaspers's distinction between these two kinds of guilt, as well as between criminal guilt and what he calls political guilt, advances our understanding of the many ways in which someone's actions, choices, and, in broader terms, their alliances, might serve as bases for different kinds of responsibility attributions.

This nuanced understanding of guilt helps to disentangle some of the confusions that arise and also captures certain stable moral intuitions, such as the intuition that those who directly participate in wrongdoing—and so are guilty in a clearly moral and perhaps also criminal sense—are differently culpable from bystanders. At the same time, we should recognize that our attraction to the distinction rests on the controversial assumption that there is a significant moral difference between choosing not to act in a way that is available and choosing to contribute to a morally reprehensible collective action. Discussions in normative moral theory show that on close inspection, the difference between what we do and what we allow to happen is not morally decisive.[3] It might be worth wondering whether all comembers are rightly understood as bystanders to wrongdoing. It is not a necessary condition of being a member of a group that one be fully apprised of all that the group does. If I am a member of a group that engages in wrongful behavior, and I fail to distance myself from the group's actions because I do not know or have reasonable grounds for knowing what the group is doing, then it would be a mistake to think of my continued membership as a choice about who I am. If this reasoning is correct, then informed comembers—bystanders of a sort—are the only ones whose continued membership or failures to speak against the group's activities make an existential statement for which they might be guilty. To the extent that it involves a choice, I claim that membership guilt is best understood as personal moral guilt, that is, guilt for one's own actions in response to the acts of a collective to which one belongs. How we position ourselves relative to a group to which we belong and which we know to act badly is a moral, not simply existential, matter. Membership guilt, while it may involve the more metaphysical notion of who we choose to be, is moral in nature as well. In the terms I have outlined in this chapter, membership guilt should be understood as a species of personal, moral guilt; it is a matter of moral responsibility at the individual level. In cases such as these, one's obligations are defined in relation to the acts of others, but one is not responsible for the others' actions. Instead, one is responsible, morally, to respond appropriately to the wrongdoing by distancing oneself from the group so far as that is possible. Failing to do so is failing to meet a moral obligation. In the moral realm, circumstances that are beyond an agent's control frequently shape the agent's obligations. Once those moral obligations are established, one becomes morally responsible in the blameworthy sense when one chooses to act against them; in short, one becomes personally guilty.

In discussing a similar sort of guilt that arises from white-skin privilege, Sandra Bartky says that "it is important to remember that there are some inequalities from which we cannot entirely divorce ourselves, no matter how hard we try."[4] Hannah Arendt discusses the "elemental shame" of being human.[5] While these discussions are secular, there is a familiar religious idea represented in this line of thought, that is, the idea that original sin leaves us all in a state of perpetual and unyielding guilt. The religious solution is God's mercy; the secular solution is less clear.

This predicament threatens to place some in the awkward position of having moral obligations as individuals—namely, the obligation to distance themselves from their communities' morally dubious behavior—that they cannot completely discharge. White people cannot, for example, do anything about their whiteness, and, more broadly, where the relevant community is all of humanity, we can never position ourselves completely outside it.

But even when someone is not voluntarily a member of a group, we will not find metaphysical guilt in the absence of moral guilt. Some might reject this claim, thinking that when membership is not voluntary and there are no exits available, moral guilt is absent because the choice aspect that many of us believe to be central to moral responsibility is absent.[6] However, as noted earlier, appropriate and inappropriate moral stances exist for individuals in blameworthy communities to take, even if leaving the community altogether is impossible. Marilyn Frye suggests, for example, that blameworthy white-skin privilege is best understood in terms of a set of behaviors and attitudes—which fall into the category of "whitely"—than as a necessary feature of being white.[7] People may not be able to shed their whiteness, but they can be morally expected to do what they can to shed their "whiteliness." This kind of approach to membership guilt makes it possible to escape; thus, agents who choose not to are for that reason culpable. I have more to say about individual moral responsibility in blameworthy communities in a later chapter.[8] For now, I want only to stress that membership guilt ought to be understood as a consequence of a significant moral choice, and so as a species of moral as well as metaphysical guilt, even where membership is involuntary. It is the failure of individuals, as individuals, to position themselves in morally appropriate ways with respect to the behavior and moral character of a blameworthy community or group of which they are members. When one is a member of a blameworthy collective, conditions exist that can have an influence on one's obligations as an individual. Understood in this sense, membership guilt is moral guilt but is not collective. It is personal guilt whose source is the failure to discharge moral obligations that arise as a result of one's association with a blameworthy collective. Though membership guilt arises in collective contexts, it is distinct from collective guilt and ought not be confused with it.

Before moving on from membership guilt, I want to draw attention to the difference between membership guilt and membership guilt feelings. Membership guilt is an objective state in which agents are morally blameworthy as a consequence of their failure to take appropriate action to distance themselves from a blameworthy collective of which they are members. It is not the same thing as the guilt feelings people sometimes experience when they feel morally tainted by the actions of comembers of a group to which they belong. For example, I may experience feelings of guilt if students from my institution conduct themselves in an unbecoming way at Homecoming and cause the local community to look unfavorably on the university. In a more urgent example, Jaspers says: "if I was present at the murder of others without risking my life to prevent it, I feel guilty in a way not adequately conceivable either legally, politically or morally. That I live after such a thing has happened weighs upon me as indelible guilt."[9] In this case, a failure to act gives rise to a subjective feeling of guilt that cannot be shaken. With respect to this guilt feeling, it makes sense to ask a further question—does our feeling of guilt have warrant when we could have prevented the moral offense? On the basis of the above discussion about bystanders as making a moral choice, the guilt feeling has warrant because I could have acted to prevent the harm. If I stand by when I could make a difference, I am guilty of an inadequate response to the acts of others. If I do not act as I ought, then my feeling of guilt is based in my recognition of my failure and warranted by the facts. Another moral possibility is that there is no obligation to intervene to the extent of risking my life. In this scenario, to do so would be supererogatory. If so, then my feeling of guilt is not supported by the moral facts of the situation. The reason it is not supported is that I am in these circumstances not guilty (in the objective sense) because I violate no moral obligation. However, unwarranted though it may be, it is still possible for me to feel guilty in this case, insofar as I have an affective response to my mistaken belief that I am guilty. In the case in which my feelings result from my sense of myself as tainted by the actions of the students who bring the university into disrepute, it is less clear that my feelings are warranted because it's less clear that I failed morally. Membership guilt may result in feelings of guilt, but if those feelings are justified, it is because of a personal failure. Earlier discussion demonstrates that, as a species of personal guilt, it is not collective. In the next section, I respond to the concern that collective guilt condemns some for the actions of others; I focus on the view that collective guilt is blameworthy moral responsibility at the collective level, and that it is different from personal guilt and membership guilt.

3.3 COLLECTIVE GUILT IS NOT DISTRIBUTIVE

Some philosophers reject the idea of collective guilt for the same reasons they reject collective moral responsibility more generally, that is, because they worry that it risks condemning some for the actions of others, thereby suggesting "injustice, vindictiveness, and the blurring of distinctions."[10] The root of such worries is the failure to distinguish between collective guilt and personal guilt. In chapter 2, we saw that this oversight leads individualists to reject collective moral responsibility altogether as anything other than a shorthand way of speaking about the moral responsibility of individuals. Earlier, we saw that collective guilt does not condemn the innocent for others' acts. Collective guilt is a feature of a collective moral agent who has acted wrongly in a blameworthy fashion. More precisely, collective guilt is collective moral responsibility in the blameworthy, as opposed to the praiseworthy, sense. My view emphasizes the importance of recognizing the distinction between the collective and individual levels of moral responsibility. A significant feature of that distinction is that ascriptions of guilt, that is, of blameworthy moral responsibility, to a collective agent do not entail that all members of the collective share in the guilt as individuals; collective guilt is not distributive. An understanding of collective moral responsibility that fails to keep these levels distinct is confused and results in premature dismissals of a significant normative concept.

The source of the confusion is the individualist idea that claims about collective action and collective moral responsibility are shorthand for more complex claims about the actions and responsibility of individuals. But how to implicate individuals in collective action situations, and what to hold them responsible for, are normative questions that we must keep distinct from questions of how to implicate collectives and what to hold them responsible for. Individualists do not recognize that a collective could be responsible in a meaningful way without holding all of its members responsible.[11] The idea of collective guilt is disturbing in the way suggested only when we believe that to ascribe guilt to a collective is to ascribe personal guilt for the collective act to every member of that collective. But, as we have seen, personal guilt and collective guilt operate at distinct levels of agency. It would be illegitimate to conclude, on the basis of an attribution of guilt to a collective, that members of the collective are equally responsible or even that every member of the collective is to some degree responsible for the collective action and its outcome. Individuals are not responsible, as individuals, for collective actions. They can, however, be responsible and, therefore, blameworthy, for their contributions to such actions.

This understanding of collective guilt as blameworthy collective moral responsibility that operates at a level distinct from individual moral responsibility flows from the claims, defended in earlier chapters, that collectives can act intentionally and that they can be morally responsible, that is, praiseworthy or blameworthy, for their actions. Collectives with the capacity for intentional action are guilty whenever they are blameworthy for their actions.

In the next section I consider collective guilt feelings.

3.4 COLLECTIVE GUILT FEELINGS

So far we have distinguished guilt from beliefs about one's guilt and from guilt feelings. We have also drawn distinctions between collective guilt and personal guilt, and established that membership guilt is best understood as a form of personal guilt. I now want to consider the notion of collective guilt feelings. There are a number of reasons for taking collective guilt feelings into consideration. First, we have already seen that collective guilt is sometimes run together with collective guilt feelings. If this happened only in the "popular" conception of guilt, it might not be worth taking philosophically seriously, since a simple clarification of the difference might disentangle the confusion.[12] But it happens also in more scholarly discussions. For example, the identification of collective guilt with collective guilt feelings is prevalent in psychological literature concerning collective guilt.[13] Second, guilt feelings might appear to play an important practical role in motivating guilty parties to act in ways appropriate to their guilt, perhaps even motivating them to repair, make amends for, or accept appropriate punishment for their wrongdoing. If guilt feelings serve this motivational function, then collective guilt feelings could be important for motivating collectives to address their guilt where apologies, reparations, and other forms of compensation are concerned. Third, it is not entirely clear what collective guilt feelings might be, since by hypothesis, collective guilt is a feature of collectives and some might be hesitant to attribute to collectives the capacity to have feelings. Many philosophers, myself included, might accept guilt feelings in the individual case but be skeptical about their existence in the collective case. Other than Margaret Gilbert's recent account of collective guilt feelings, which I consider shortly, there are no well-developed philosophical theories of collective guilt feelings. Psychological accounts are not consistent with the view of collective guilt developed so far in this chapter; instead they characterize them as feelings of membership guilt (whether warranted or not). An additional reason for taking collective guilt feelings into account is that some might think that guilt feelings are morally appropriate responses to a self-assessment of guilt, and that agents who fail to experience feelings of guilt while believing themselves to be guilty fall short in moral terms. If collectives cannot feel guilty, then perhaps they lack an important moral capacity.

Let me begin the discussion of collective guilt feelings by asking whether we should be skeptical of collective guilt feelings. The answer is yes. In order to remain consistent with the view defended in this book, collective guilt feelings need to be feelings of a collective, not of individual members of the collective. Just as collective guilt is a feature of the collective and so differs from personal guilt, collective guilt feelings are different from personal guilt feelings because the former are feelings of the collective. Unless we distinguish feelings from their sensations—a move that Gilbert makes and that I argue ought to be avoided—collectives just do not appear to be the sorts of things that can have feelings. Even as highly structured a collective as a corporation "has no soul to damn, no body to kick,"[14] and, we might add, no body with which to experience sensations.

The conflation of collective guilt with collective guilt feelings is most apparent in the psychological literature on collective guilt, which, arguably, is wholly concerned with collective guilt as an emotional response. However, in the terms of our discussion, this understanding of collective guilt is not in any substantive sense collective. Consider the description with which Nyla R. Branscombe and Bertjan Doosje begin their anthology *Collective Guilt*: "Collective guilt stems from the distress that group members experience when they accept that their in-group is responsible for immoral actions that harmed another group. It is a self-conscious emotion that can occur when the individual's collective identity or association with a group whose actions are perceived as immoral is salient. . . . Because collective guilt is a psychological experience, it need not involve actually being guilty in any sense of the word."[15] These authors are quite clearly talking about guilt feelings. It is less clear, however, whether these feelings are collective. Instead, they appear to be feelings that individuals experience based on their association with a blameworthy collective. These feelings are not, in the terms I have outlined here, feelings of collective guilt, because it is individuals who experience them in response to their own personal guilt. Thus, we may set aside the psychologists' discussion of collective guilt as collective guilt feelings since, strictly speaking, they are not collective guilt feelings and they do not constitute collective guilt as we are understanding it, that is, as blameworthy moral responsibility at the collective level.

Let us now consider whether collective guilt feelings serve a significant normative purpose. They might play a motivational role in getting members of collectives to respond appropriately to collective guilt. If we think that guilt feelings are important in this respect, then we need an account of them at the collective level that addresses our initial skepticism concerning collectives' capacity to experience feelings. Gilbert believes that collective guilt feelings serve a particular and useful function, insofar as they commit individuals who constitute the collective to act in certain ways. For example, they would characterize the group's relevant act as wrong and they would ascribe guilt feelings to the group. Moreover, collective guilt feelings would "help to ameliorate relations between wrongfully acting collectives, their victims, and others. They would also be apt to improve the relevant collectives themselves."[16] Collective guilt feelings indicate an acknowledgment, on the collective's part, of its wrongdoing.

Gilbert uses her plural subject theory as a framework for her account of collective guilt. Understanding her view of collective guilt feelings requires a basic understanding of her notions of joint commitment and plural subject. I briefly outline them here. Though there is a lot to say about the plural subject theory, I here limit critical evaluation to Gilbert's discussion of collective guilt feelings. Fundamental to Gilbert's plural subject theory is the notion of a joint commitment. According to her account, joint commitments have normative force. They are not aggregates of personal commitments. Gilbert says, "Those initiating such a commitment do not each create a part of it by making a personal decision. Rather, they participate in creating the whole of it along with the other parties. A joint commitment does not have parts, though it certainly has implications for individual parties. That is, they are committed through the joint commitment."[17]

Once in place, the joint commitment binds each individual who is party to it. They are committed to following through. A group of people constitutes a plural subject when they are jointly committed to doing something "as a body." Using this framework, Gilbert characterizes collective guilt feelings in the following way: "For us collectively to feel guilt over our action A is for us to constitute the plural subject of a feeling of guilt over our action A."[18] This amounts to the parties committing to act so as to constitute a single, unified subject of guilt feelings. Once the commitment is in play, individuals are required to act in ways appropriate to it. Among other things, this means that "they will refrain from proposing that it is morally acceptable for the group to engage in an obviously similar action" and "should one of their number propose such a thing, they will feel free to remonstrate with the person in question."[19] These commitments are analogous to what we might expect of an individual who feels guilty. If someone did not act in a way that was appropriate to feeling guilt, we would not believe that she had feelings of guilt. Using parallel reasoning, Gilbert supposes that collective guilt feelings require certain behaviors if they are to be credible.[20]

On this account, collective guilt feelings have functional descriptions and do not have a collective affective component. That is, they are feelings, but they are not experienced as sensations by the collective that has them. In this way, Gilbert addresses the skeptical concern that collectives are not the sorts of things that can experience feelings. Her account allows that they can have them when parties enact a joint commitment to feel guilt as a body, but does not require that the plural subject feel the collective guilt feeling.

It is worth repeating that the relevant behaviors that flow from the joint commitment are required by, not just evidence of, a collective guilt feeling. In essence, collective guilt feelings play the role of providing individuals with reasons for action that have normative force because of their source in commitments. We may, indeed, understand collective guilt as generating obligations for individual members of the collective. Because agents, including collective agents, may be guilty without being aware of it or acknowledging it, collective guilt in the absence of collective guilt feelings cannot fulfill the same function. Moreover, given their normative impact on individuals within collectives, Gilbert maintains that collective guilt feelings "would help to ameliorate relations between wrongfully acting collectives, their victims, and others" and "[t]hey would also be apt to improve the relevant collectives themselves."[21] Thus, according to Gilbert, collective guilt feelings are normatively significant. Is she correct?

I take issue with Gilbert on two points in particular. First, I reject her characterization of the collective acknowledgment of guilt as a "collective guilt feeling." Second, I question the analogy between collective guilt feelings and personal guilt feelings that Gilbert uses throughout her account. I take these points up in order.

Consider the personal case. We can see that at the personal level, an acknowledgment of guilt is not the same thing as a guilt feeling. Individuals may acknowledge their guilt in different ways, and feeling guilty may be one way of acknowledging guilt. But it is not the only way. I may acknowledge my guilt by attempting to compensate the wronged party or parties, by apologizing for my behavior, or by promising to do things differently in the future. All of these are acknowledgments of a sort, and none requires that I feel guilty. Similarly, in the collective case, it is possible for collectives and members of collectives to act in ways that acknowledge their guilt without feeling guilty. Gilbert's central idea, that there could be a joint commitment collectively to acknowledge wrongdoing and to act in ways appropriate to that acknowledgment, has practical merits because it places normative constraints on what collectives and their members are to do when they "feel guilty." It is a mistake, however, to call the acknowledgment of collective guilt a "collective guilt feeling," particularly while removing the affective aspect from it. It is a mistake because an insistence on the language of collective guilt feelings could lead many to reject the otherwise plausible collective phenomenon of acknowledging collective guilt. Collective concepts face enough opposition without invoking language that misleads in ways that then need to be explained away. Instead, we would do better to set aside the language and idea of collective guilt feelings, and focus on collective guilt itself as a species of collective moral responsibility. Given the distinctions outlined earlier between being guilty, believing oneself to be guilty, and feeling guilty, it is perfectly plausible that collectives might (1) be guilty and (2) believe themselves to be guilty but (3) not feel guilty. Such a state would not in the least impede a collective's ability to acknowledge and respond to its moral blameworthiness.

Gilbert takes collective guilt feelings to be analogous in important ways to personal guilt feelings, so it is worth considering the extent to which they are similar and whether there are significant ways they differ from one another. The range of behaviors that Gilbert associates with collective guilt feelings is meant to mirror the range of behaviors we would expect of someone experiencing personal guilt feelings.[22] A significant disanalogy between personal guilt feelings and collective guilt feelings is that individuals do not respond to personal guilt feelings because they are required to; personal guilt feelings do not obligate us or commit us to taking a particular course of action. Rather, if these feelings have a practical function it is their motivational role, insofar as the associated unease promises to lift if the party experiencing personal guilt acts in ways that acknowledge that guilt. Uncomfortable feelings prod us in the direction of right action, that is, they motivate us to do the right thing. But being motivated is not the same thing as having an obligation. An agent may have an obligation and be aware of that obligation, yet nonetheless lack the motivation to act on it. If the main role of collective guilt feelings in the plural subject account is to commit or obligate individuals who are party to the agreement to feel guilt as a body, then the same role could easily be fulfilled by less elaborate means, that is, by an agreement to acknowledge guilt as a body. However, if the main role of collective guilt feelings in the plural subject account is to motivate individuals to act in ways appropriate to that guilt and a simple acknowledgment will not suffice, then it looks as if, on the analogue with personal guilt, the feelings are best not dissociated from the sensation of them, since that is what gets the agent moving.

Given Gilbert's emphasis on the joint commitment that collective guilt feelings effect, it is fair to say that their main function is to obligate, not so much to motivate, the parties to the joint commitment. However, this view introduces a complication of its own. The difficulty stems from a consideration of why the phenomenon of feelings is at all significant in matters of guilt, collective or otherwise. In the personal case, as noted, if guilt feelings are normatively important, it is not as mere epiphenomena, but instead because of their motivational role. If they did not play that role, then they would not be normatively interesting, though they might be psychologically interesting. Thus, if we jettison the notion that guilt feelings function in a motivational role, then the very intuition that warrants our initial interest in them falls away. Furthermore, as we have seen, if collective guilt feelings gain significance because they create commitments, then they are quite different in nature from the personal guilt feelings to which they are being compared and from which comparison they gain plausibility. Either they motivate, in which case they need to be felt, or they obligate, in which case they are not sufficiently analogous to personal guilt feelings to gain credibility through a comparison with them.

A final consideration that is in favor of collective guilt feelings, but that Gilbert does not entertain, is that guilt feelings may be considered morally appropriate responses to self-assessments of guilt.[23] One might argue that if an agent does not respond with guilt feelings, then the agent falls morally short. If collectives cannot have guilt feelings, then on this view they consistently fall short as moral agents whenever they are guilty. The more significant threat would be that their failure on this front might altogether call into question the possibility of collective agency if the capacity for appropriate affective responses to moral guilt is a prerequisite for moral agency. In earlier chapters, I have argued that the capacity for intentional action is the main requirement for moral agency. Thus, collectives' agency is not in question simply because they are incapable of experiencing affect. Some might press the point, however, claiming that collectives are lesser agents because of this incapacity. Two responses make sense here. First, even if moral feelings show something virtuous about moral agents, they are not the only indicators of moral virtue. As we have seen, morally appropriate feelings do not exhaust the range of morally appropriate responses to self-assessments of guilt. Collectives are capable of acknowledging their guilt in a variety of ways, and it is not clear that their inability to feel guilt makes them lesser in an agency sense. Second, beyond intentional agency, it is not obvious that all moral agents must have exactly the same capacities. We might say that collective agents are different from, not lesser than, individual agents. Such a claim would hardly be controversial; of course they are different. But they still satisfy the conditions for moral agency. It is also worth noting that the claim of lesser agency gains currency only if we insist that moral feelings constitute an important part of moral agency. And while

Kant is good company for those who might deny the significance of moral feelings in moral agency, we do not need to endorse the Kantian view that feelings undermine the moral quality of our actions to allow that moral action is possible in the absence of feelings. These considerations mitigate against the view that collective agency is compromised if collectives are incapable of collective guilt feelings.

In summary, collective guilt feelings are not required for an adequate collective acknowledgment of collective guilt, and the language of feelings is a poor choice. Furthermore, the significant disanalogy between collective and personal guilt feelings, given the assumption that collectives do not feel these feelings and so are not motivated to act on them in the same way that individuals are motivated to act on personal guilt feelings, calls the normative significance of collective guilt feelings into question. Finally, it is not the case that collectives' incapacity to experience collective guilt feelings calls their agency into question. I suggest, therefore, that collective guilt feelings are not required in order to fill in any gap between collective guilt and its acknowledgment, and that an adequate account of collective guilt does not require an account of collective guilt feelings.

3.5 CONCLUSION

My goal has been to explicate the notion of collective guilt as blameworthy collective moral responsibility. Understood in this way, collective guilt is different from personal guilt and from membership guilt (which is a species of personal guilt). Collective guilt is also distinct from collectives' beliefs about their guilt and from collective guilt feelings, which I have shown to be an unnecessary addition to the normative understanding of collective guilt. In establishing this last claim, I considered Gilbert's functional account of collective guilt feelings and maintained that we could capture the essential idea of collective acknowledgment of guilt without complicating the matter with the notion of collective guilt feelings. Though some people have tended to confuse collective guilt with feelings of collective guilt, it is not the case that collective guilt is a feeling, and it is not the case that the feelings that are frequently associated with collective guilt are feelings attributable to collectives. Hence, according to my view, these feelings are not properly characterized as collective guilt feelings. Much confusion concerning collective guilt and the feelings that members of collectives experience when they are associated with a blameworthy collective has resulted from the failure to distinguish adequately between collective and individual levels of moral responsibility. When we keep this distinction and what follows from it firmly in mind, and remember that collective guilt is fundamentally blameworthy moral responsibility at the collective level, we can see that the notion of collective guilt is not nearly as complicated or troubling as some have made it out to be.

PART TWO

INDIVIDUAL MORAL
RESPONSIBILITY IN
COLLECTIVE CONTEXTS

[4]

INDIVIDUAL RESPONSIBILITY FOR (AND IN) COLLECTIVE WRONGS

The view developed so far—that collective intention, collective action, and collective moral responsibility operate at the level of collectives—suggests that individuals are not responsible for collective actions as such. Specifically, it suggests that, insofar as collective wrongdoing is the fault of a collective agent, not of an individual human agent, individuals are not blameworthy for it. If this is the case, then the two-level view might appear to result in a normative loss because it seems to absolve individuals of responsibility in collective wrongdoing. The main purpose of this chapter is to address this concern. I address it in two ways. First, I evaluate its accuracy. Perhaps under some conditions, individuals can be responsible for collective actions. If agents may at times be responsible for the actions of others, then it is possible that in some circumstances an individual human agent might be morally responsible for a collective act even though the agent of that act in question is a collective agent, not the individual human agent whose responsibility is in question. Exploring this possibility will in particular account for situations in which authority structures in organizations authorize individual human agents to act on behalf of the organization. It is tempting to think that the acts of, for example, heads of state, chief executive officers, and presidents of universities might be understood in this manner. I resist this conclusion, while at the same time taking seriously the idea that the authority conferred on individuals by the formal structures of an organization makes some individuals more responsible than others. Second, I distinguish between responsibility for collective action and responsibility in collective action, and argue throughout that although individuals are not morally responsible, as individuals, for collective action, we have good reason to think they can be morally responsible in collective action. My task, then, is to provide an account of individual responsibility in the context of collective action.

Recall the distinction made in chapter 1 between organizations and goal-oriented collective agents. These do not exhaust the kinds of entities we may wish to consider collectives because, as noted earlier, some collectives may not be agents at all. Since I focus on moral responsibility, I attend only to the two kinds of collectives that qualify as agents: organizations and goal-oriented collectives. Organizations are highly structured collectives with formal mechanisms for making decisions, articulating the collective's goals and interests, and outlining the positions of individuals within the structure. Goal-oriented collectives coalesce around action toward the achievement of a particular goal that the members jointly embrace and aspire to. The intentional structures of these two types of collective agent are sufficiently different from each other to merit different treatment. Given this difference, in cases of collective wrongdoing the roles and responsibilities of individuals in organizations merit being analyzed differently from those of individuals in goal-oriented collectives. For this reason, I take up the two types separately here, just as I did when I discussed their intentional structures in chapter 1.

First, I address responsibility in organizations. I explore the strong intuition that leaders in organizations are responsible as individuals for the actions of the organizations because their actions just are the actions of the organization. I argue that this intuition is close to but does not hit the mark. We look to the leaders not because their acts are the acts of the organization, but rather because the organization empowers them to act in ways that they would not be able to but for their roles in the structure. Second, I address responsibility in goal-oriented collectives. I argue that individual contributors to the intentional actions of goal-oriented collectives are responsible for their contributions. I maintain further that their contributions need to be understood in the context of the collective action of which they are parts.

Before I get to that discussion, I want to provide two bits of background. The first is about the distinction between collective wrongdoing and collective or cumulative harm. The second concerns an account of action description that is pertinent to my analysis. I address both in the following section.

4.1 BACKGROUND

What is the difference between collective wrongdoing and collective harm? When a collective agent performs a collective action that violates a moral principle, then that action constitutes a collective wrongdoing. The agent, except where it has a defensible excuse, is blameworthy for that action. Most wrongdoing also constitutes harm. I am not just wronged but also harmed when you steal from me, murder me, or discriminate against me on the basis of the color of my skin. However, many harms involve no wrongdoing. When I'm injured in a mudslide, I am harmed but not wronged. If someone slices her finger with a paring knife, she suffers harm but is not wronged. In the collective case, the cumulative impact of parallel individual actions may result in collective harm that is not the result of collective wrongdoing, that is, of the wrongdoing of a collective agent. For example, humanity's environmental impact on the world is surely harmful. However, it would be a conceptual stretch to claim that it is the work of a collective agent. I draw particular attention to the difference between collective wrongdoing and collective or cumulative harms, because running these together creates confusion when we are attempting to decipher the relationship between individual responsibility and collective wrongdoing. In situations in which collective agency is absent, moral responsibility, if present at all, resides only at the level of individuals. Many cases of cumulative harm have this character—the harm itself occurs only because of the actions of a number of people. Individual contributions to it, taken on their own, might involve no or negligible harm. Environmental harm such as that which has resulted in climate change might be viewed in this way. In the following chapters, I'll talk about the collective and individual responses required in these sorts of cases. For the time being, my goal is only to highlight the distinction between wrongdoing and harm so that it will not confuse my discussion of individual moral responsibility in collective wrongdoing.

I now turn to a brief overview of action descriptions. It is an important part of my view that the moral rightness or wrongness, praiseworthiness or blameworthiness of individual actions in collective contexts derives from the relationship between the individual's action and the collective action or situation. Acts of individual human agents may be described in ways that draw attention to the collective features of the situations in which they take place. Drawing on an earlier example, running a race may have no moral content when considered in isolation, but when it is part of a large fundraiser, we highlight its moral contours whenever we describe it as such, for example, as raising money for cancer research. The view of action description on which I depend is familiar from Donald Davidson's influential work. Davidson claims that the same act particular or token may be described in multiple ways, that is, it might instantiate more than one act-type.[1] Different descriptions provide different information about the same act. Thus, to use Davidson's example, consider a case in which I flip a switch. Flipping the switch may have a number of consequences. If by doing so I alert a burglar, turn on the light, open the electrical current, wake up the neighbors, and so on, then my act may be redescribed in these different ways. In much the same way as when we describe one person in different ways—"the author of this book," "the philosopher in Stevenson Hall 3138," "the host of the Researching Women conference"—we may do the same where acts are concerned. A given act may be described as "a switch-flipping," "an alerting of the burglar," "a moving of my index finger," or "a turning on of the lights."[2] With respect to action descriptions, Joel Feinberg called this expanding and contracting to include more or less information about consequences "the accordion effect."[3]

Normative facts may be among the information contained in a description of an action, especially when we invoke a description that falls into the category of what Bernard Williams calls "thick moral terms." Thick moral terms, such as "stealing" and "murder," have moral evaluations built into them or are at least suggestive of particular moral judgments.[4] For example, when I flip the switch I might also detonate an explosive. When I detonate an explosive, I might also kill a rival. If I kill the rival intentionally, then the killing is a murder. When we describe it as such, we invoke a description with moral resonance: we recognize that acts warranting the description "murder" are wrong. That's what makes "murder" a thick moral term. We do not describe accidental killings or justified killings in the same way. Though they result in death, they do not qualify as murders.

I draw attention to this theory of action descriptions and the accordion effect in order to introduce a simple point: the action of an individual may warrant descriptions that invoke collective content. In some situations, this collective content may, as in the individual case, make reference to act descriptions that guide us to moral judgments. I have made this point a number of times with respect to the redescription of running a race as "raising funds for cancer research." Fundraising for cancer is clearly a laudable activity in both its individual and collective forms.

Recalling my discussion of the prevalence of our understanding of genocide as a mass atrocity, it is another scenario that draws attention to collective misdeeds. An individual act of murder, performed as a part of a larger initiative of genocide, has a distinct moral character that it would lack outside the genocidal context because in genocide it is performed with the aim of destroying a group. When we describe it as a contribution to genocide, we draw attention to that moral feature of it. I shall return to these points later in this chapter, when I discuss individual responsibility in the context of the intentional actions of goal-oriented collective agents.

4.2 INDIVIDUAL MORAL RESPONSIBILITY IN ORGANIZATIONAL WRONGDOING

The following question guides my discussion in this chapter: when individuals take part in collective wrongdoing, for what are they responsible—the collective wrong as such or something else, such as their contribution to it? First, let me be clear that I understand collective wrongdoing as the wrongdoing of a collective agent, either an organization or a goal-oriented collective. If collective wrongdoing takes place in the absence of a collective excuse—understanding an excuse as a reason that justifies the behavior and alleviates blameworthiness—then the collective agent is blameworthy. Given a two-level understanding of moral responsibility as operating at the level of individuals and the level of collectives, it is not clear how this evaluation of blameworthiness in a collective agent should inform our evaluation of the actions of individuals. As mentioned earlier in this chapter, some people worry that, having made an attribution of collective moral responsibility, we give up the possibility of meaningfully attributing moral responsibility to individuals. I maintain that we do not. To see why, let us begin with a case of collective wrongdoing involving an organization.

Recall the case of the Canadian Red Cross and their handling, or rather mishandling, of the Canadian blood supply. As a result of a poor system using outdated methods of testing that did not adequately reveal the presence of HIV and hepatitis C in blood and blood products, over two thousand Canadians contracted HIV, and sixty thousand contracted hepatitis C over the course of a decade from medical interventions such as blood transfusions.[5] The Canadian Red Cross is a large nonprofit organization whose major activities used to include taking, processing, and distributing blood donations for hospitals across the country. A public inquiry headed by Judge Horace Krever of the Ontario Court of Appeal revealed that a series of bad decisions made by Red Cross executives contributed to many unnecessary infections and deaths by way of the blood supply. Hemophiliacs were the most vulnerable group, because they depend on regular transfusions of concentrated blood product in order to survive. The decisions with fatal consequences include (but are by no means limited to) the decision not to screen blood donors or single out high-risk groups, the decision not to switch hemophiliacs to a safer, nonconcentrated product, and a general resistance to growing evidence in the early 1980s that AIDS was a blood-borne disease.[6] Moreover, when test kits that could detect HIV in blood became available, "bureaucratic niceties—meetings, budget approval, contracts, training, staffing—proceeded as if the purchase was for office supplies," with the result that at least 133 transfusion recipients became infected during the approvals process.[7] Given that the distribution of infected blood through the 1980s is considered to be the worst public health disaster the country has ever experienced, it is a wonder that decisions at the time were taken with such leisure. The outcome of the inquiry into this dark time was that the Canadian Red Cross is no longer permitted to collect and distribute blood and blood products in Canada. Judge Krever also named particular individuals, whom he identified as "people in positions of responsibility who failed in their duties, oftentimes with fatal consequences."[8]

The scope of the Red Cross's activities means that it had, at the time, many levels of roles and responsibility, a number of portfolios in addition to its responsibility for blood and blood products, and mechanisms for making decisions and carrying them out. It is thus a collective agent in the organizational sense, and we can understand the contamination of the blood supply as its (collective) moral failure. What about the individuals involved? In what follows, I consider the means by which we might attribute responsibility to individuals in the context of collective moral failure and transgression. I do this by looking at involvement of two different kinds of individual. First, people who are in executive roles that are defined by their authority to make or contribute to key organizational decisions are likely to be implicated in organizational wrongdoing. Second, people who are employees whose positions are defined in task-oriented ways that simply carry out the business of the organization as required by its structures, policies, and decisions have far less influence and are less likely—albeit not entirely unlikely—to be implicated in organizational wrongdoing. Note that the discussion that follows applies only to individual responsibility in organizational contexts; individual moral responsibility in the context of goal-oriented collectives warrants a somewhat different analysis because the structural features of the collective agent are different, thus issuing in a different relationship between the whole and the individuals within it.

In his discussion of crimes against humanity, Larry May maintains that one way of holding individuals responsible for group wrongs is to establish that a collective entity, such as a state, is responsible, and then turn our attention to the individuals who play the most significant role(s) in the collective structure.[9] This model works well for organizations and speaks to the possibility of holding individuals, such as key decision-makers, responsible in the collective wrongdoing of the Red Cross. If, for example, the final decision about whether to pull or use a shipment of blood that was known to be contaminated was in the hands of one individual, then that individual's decision to use the blood to make factor concentrate for the treatment of hemophiliacs may be redescribed as the decision of the Red Cross.[10] It is attractive and compelling to think that when such is the case, the individual is morally responsible for exactly what the Red Cross is morally responsible for: the intentional use of contaminated blood in the face of alternatives that would have reduced the risks. There are two ways such an analysis of the situation might gain currency. First, its strength might lie in the claim that the individual's act just is the act of the organization. Second, the plausibility of the analysis might reside in the claim that an individual's power is made possible by her or his role as defined by the organizational structures. I take them up in turn and argue that the second way has more promise.

Especially when one individual is the sole decision-maker for an organization, it is tempting to think that the individual's actions and decisions, or at least the subset of them required by the individual's role, are the actions and decisions of the collective agent. Another way of putting it is that the intentions and actions of the individual may be redescribed as the intentions and actions of the collective— that is, something like the accordion effect could be at work. On closer inspection, however, this understanding turns out to be an oversimplification of the case. Consider an earlier example. When I switch on a light and also, in the same act, alert the burglar, then we may redescribe my act of switching on the light as "my alerting the burglar." Both descriptions are descriptions of my own act. The same agent is the subject of each description. Now consider the redescription in the Red Cross case. The agent makes an executive decision to use the contaminated blood products. In our redescription, we redescribe his decision to do so as "the Red Cross's decision to use the contaminated products." This redescription is different from the typical redescription with the accordion effect, because the subject of the action changes, whereas the description of the act itself does not. Redescriptions typically give us more information about the consequences of the action, for example if by turning on the light I alerted the burglar, then my act had two consequences: the light went on and the burglar was alerted. The act expands and contracts, something like an accordion, depending on how it is described. In these cases, the same act token bears several descriptions. The relationship between my turning on the light and my alerting the burglar is an identity relationship. That is not the same as a case in which the executive's act is redescribed as the act of the organization. As we saw earlier when discussing the intentional structure of an organization, an individual's decision does not yield an organizational action all on its own. In the Red Cross case, for example, if a sole decision-maker determined the course of the organization, then that person's decisions would only translate into organizational decisions and action in the context of the organization's formal structures, role responsibilities, and mechanisms for acting. The individual's authority to make the organization's decisions depends entirely on her or his role and the structures that empower that role. The capacities of the individual combine with these other features of the organization to generate the organization's intentional actions. What the individual does—for example, make a decision—is only partly constitutive of what the collective does. Its relationship to the collective act is not an identity relation. An additional reason for rejecting the identity claim between the individual's actions and the organization's is the now familiar point, highlighted by the facts of the organizational structure, that the individual's personal intentions are different in content and in structure from the collective intentions of the organization. If intentions cause actions and if identical actions have identical causal origins, then this fact alone casts doubt on the claim that an individual agent's decisions and actions are the same as the decisions and actions of an organization, regardless of the individual's role.

But establishing an identity between an individual's acts and those of an organization is not the only way of establishing individual moral responsibility in the context of organizational wrongdoing. The preceding discussion helps to show that our belief that individuals in positions of authority are responsible for the actions of the organization gains strength when we note that the individual would not be able to do what she or he does if not for occupying the role. Some roles confer powers that individuals would not otherwise have, and the context of collective agency gives those powers scope and reach that they would otherwise lack. For this reason, individuals have influence that brings with it responsibility.

Given these considerations, not only are there grounds for holding people in positions of power responsible as individuals for the consequences of their decisions, but we have reasons for holding the actions taken by individuals in these roles to a higher moral standard than those taken in the absence of these roles. This heightened responsibility responds to the worry that collective agency dilutes individual responsibility. Rather than diluting individual responsibility in these cases, the context of collective responsibility actually increases it. Decision-makers for organizations must be regarded as responsible for the decisions they make—blameworthy for blameworthy decisions, praiseworthy for praiseworthy decisions—not because their actions and decisions are the actions and decisions of the organization, but because outside their role, their actions and decisions would not have the impact they do. This view does not commit us to the claim that these individual human agents are, in a literal sense, performing collective actions as individual human agents or that their actions are identical to the actions of the organization. While I have provided some reasons for skepticism concerning the identity claim between authorized individual acts and acts of an organization, the metaphysical point need not be settled here. What it does entail is that the individual's actions in the role have the full force of an empowering organizational structure behind them and the individual has a moral obligation to take them with this in mind. If it turned out that one individual had been responsible for every decision the Red Cross made about the blood supply, then that individual would be blameworthy for her or his part—that is, for making decisions that resulted in preventable deaths. But the individual's responsibility does not take the place of the organizational responsibility of the Red Cross. Similarly, if an executive committee reached key decisions, the members' authority would raise the stakes of individual moral responsibility in their performance of their roles. But this would not take the place of the responsibility of the organization because that is grounded in the intentional structure of the organization, namely, that which grounds its agency.

May suggests a further reason for implicating leaders in collective responsibility. He says of heads of state in state-sponsored genocide that "while it is true that [they] normally do not do the deeds of murder, rape, or torture themselves, these acts would not occur [as crimes of the state] but for the direction of the leaders."[11] May suggests that we should think of the leaders as "setting" the intentions of the state. In an organizational context, we may think of the leader or the executive body making the organization's decisions in much the same way. Think of the Red Cross, as we did above, as having an executive committee that decides how the organization will do its business. This committee functions much as heads of state would. The organization acts in ways that are consistent with what the leader or leaders want for it. In the case of the Red Cross, its leaders set an agenda of proceeding conservatively when more proactive, rigorous policies would have had a life-saving impact. As May explains with respect to international crime, conceptually it makes sense to think of the leader as "setting" the intentions of the organization. As a result, the leader will be the easiest to implicate when something goes wrong. Once collective wrongdoing has been established, the leader's role or leaders' roles in the organization secures her or his (or their) moral responsibility as well. According to this view, individuals in leadership roles can be responsible for collective wrongs as collective wrongs, not just for the consequences of their actions as individuals, because they set the intentions of the organization and set in motion collective actions on the basis of those intentions.

This is a plausible view insofar as collectives' intentions ground their agency and, if this view is correct, leaders determine what those intentions will be, at least in some circumstances. I believe that the influence leaders have over organizational directions and intentions heightens and extends their responsibility, as was just articulated. At the same time, the formal policies and structures also contribute by setting both content and process restrictions on how those in positions of power may carry out their roles. Only in the rarest cases does an individual have absolute power to set the intentions of the organization. When this happens, May is right to claim that it provides a strong reason for holding individuals responsible for organizational action. The reason is not an identity between the individual's acts and the organizational acts, but rather the manner in which the organization's intentional acts flow as consequences from the actions and decisions of the individual leader. Even when these conditions do not obtain, however, we see that the empowering nature of the organizational structure increases the individual responsibility of agents who are so empowered such that they are responsible as individuals for their far-reaching contributions, and these contributions might have as a direct consequence morally wrong action at the collective level.

If individuals in positions of power are in some measure responsible for the moral failings of the organization itself, then we might wonder anew what the point is of insisting on the moral responsibility of the organization at the collective level. Note that my goal in this section is to articulate how individuals may be morally responsible in collective wrongdoing. Earlier chapters have focused on explaining the nature of collective agency, how organizational structures give rise to intentional collective action, and why we should understand those actions as the products of collective agency. The concern this discussion of individual moral responsibility in collective wrongdoing is meant to address is the concern that if we countenance collective moral agency, it will eclipse individual moral agency in these situations. The objection under discussion now goes the other way, claiming that once we account for individuals as morally responsible—perhaps through their leadership roles and the parts they play in decision-making and in setting the direction and intentions of the organization—collective moral responsibility is no longer necessary. One reason for thinking that it is necessary is that in an organizational setting, decisions are sometimes made that no one would make alone. Philip Pettit, for one, has argued that certain joint decision-making processes can yield outcomes different from the wishes of the individuals whose expressed preferences factor into the decision. Pettit's claim rests on the existence of what he calls "discursive dilemmas," which seems to indicate that attitudes of organizations are not simply a function of the attitudes of their members.[12] As noted earlier, collectives, for example the Department of Philosophy's hiring committee, sometimes reach decisions that none of the individuals would make if given the executive power to decide alone. These decisions are truly collective, arising from the intentional structures of the collective as outlined in my earlier discussion of intentional collective agency. This feature of collective decision-making helps to show the distinct character of collective intentions in much the same way that their difference from leaders' personal intentions does. In both instances, the intentions and decisions of the organization operate as distinct phenomena whose content is not necessarily a function of the content of the personal intentions of individuals or even of their individual aims and desires for the organization. Moreover, apart from the existence of collective decisions that do not reflect what any one individual would choose alone, note that even when leaders in an organization set its intentions and interests, they do so under constraint of existing organizational policies, interests, attitudes, practices, and culture. This feature of an organization's intentional structure explains why a collective's intentions are distinct from the personal intentions of its members.

Given this understanding of individual responsibility in contexts of organizational agency, we can see that workers who are not in leadership roles will not be responsible for their roles in organizational actions in the same way. If there is any possibility for them to be responsible, then it needs to be on different grounds. Their actions might well contribute to the actions of the collective, yet at the same time their roles are much more those of cogs in the organizational machinery. Consider the Red Cross workers whose job it was to take blood from donors at blood clinics. If not for their actions within the organization, contaminated blood would not have been collected and distributed in such quantities. But, assuming collective wrongdoing, does their role in the organizational wrongdoing implicate them at the individual level? In my discussion of the intentional structure of organizational agency, I maintained that individuals performing their roles in organizations may do so without sharing any commitment to the overall goals and interests of the organization. Organizations act when people within them perform their functions in their roles, but because of the formal structures in the organizational setting, it is not the case that a commitment to a shared goal is needed in order for the organization to act. The cohesiveness of the actions—their identity as actions of the organization—comes from the policies, procedures, role definition, and structures of authority. What is more, it is possible that some of the workers who took blood were fully alienated from the organization's broader goals. They might well have been working only for the paycheck or because they simply liked interacting with people every day. Yet their everyday activities in the workplace contributed to a tremendously tragic collective wrong. But, given their roles, they had no reason to concern themselves with the broader interests and intentions that governed the policies and processes framing their work. And more than that, there is no reason to think of them as blameworthy for lacking a broader view. Rank-and-file workers are not morally required to investigate every aspect of the organization in which they function. Despite their contributions to the overall wrongdoing, these individuals are not morally responsible for it or for their contributions to it. They are not morally responsible for the collective wrongdoing because they neither set the goals and intentions of the organization (as the executives do) nor have much knowledge of or commitment to those goals.

We can imagine a case in which a worker becomes personally disgruntled and sets out to sabotage the blood supply. If this were a personal decision, not in compliance with a broader organizational decision, then this individual would be morally responsible for her or his actions and for the contamination of the blood supply, but not in the context of organizational policy. Instead, we should then understand her or him as acting alone rather than as doing something as part of an organizational endeavor.

Finally, it will not of course be the case that every single worker who does not have the power to contribute to organizational decisions is thoroughly ignorant of or uninterested in the broader organizational goals. For example, in the context of organizational nonchalance about harm-producing risks to the blood supply, there may be cases of lower level workers who are well aware that they are dealing with contaminated blood yet do nothing to stop it or, more egregiously, are zealous in their compliance with what they know to be inadequate policy. Are these individuals, insofar as they share in and intentionally act toward the organizational aims, morally responsible as individuals for the organizational wrongdoing as such? I maintain that they are not. Their limited power within the organization removes them from responsibility for the collective wrongdoing as a whole. But these individuals are not blameless in this situation either. Their blameworthiness has two sources. First, they are blameworthy for their personal contributions to a morally problematic collective goal. Second, they are blameworthy for their failure to do anything to stop the situation or, if they were completely powerless to stop it, for their failure to distance themselves appropriately from the wrongdoing, either by calling it into question or refusing to participate, even if such acts of distancing might result in their losing their jobs. I address these in turn in what follows.

With respect to individuals being responsible for their contributions to morally problematic collective goals taken in an organizational context where they have little power over organizational direction, policy, and intention, recall that we are focusing on individuals who are committed to the morally questionable goal. It makes sense to think that individuals are at least responsible for what they do in the service of collective wrongdoing; but we might think that this limited attribution of responsibility will not implicate individuals much at all. In some cases, the harm of one individual's contributions might seem negligible in the scheme of things. For example, this one employee might take only a small fraction of blood for the national supply, and only a small portion of that fraction might be dangerous. On its own, this contribution would not be enough to create much risk and certainly not enough to produce a contaminated blood supply that poses a national threat to public health. This strategy could, therefore, involve a rather sharp retreat from the one extreme of considering this kind of participant responsible for the entire organizational wrongdoing to the other extreme of considering her or him responsible for such a small contribution that it scarcely matters. I think this concern—that people will not be held sufficiently responsible for what they do in the service of collective wrongdoing—is exaggerated. Since we may accurately describe this individual's actions as intentional contributions to collective wrongdoing, the smallness of the contribution does not detract from its overall nature as a wrong. Is it a monumental wrong? No, it is not. Again, in the context of the overall effort, it is only a small part. As described, this individual has limited power and is in no position to influence organizational policy or determine the organization's intentions. It is fitting that people in more authoritative roles should, in virtue of their powers within the organization, be considered more responsible since their own contributions serve the collective ends more centrally. Neither individual is responsible for collective wrongdoing as such. However, they are responsible in different degrees to the extent that their contributions, powers, and influence are differently related to the overall goals. The vigor with which employees with little influence carry out their duties does not alter their situation within the power structure. This source of blameworthiness, that is, blameworthiness resulting from the contribution to the collective wrongdoing, is just one reason for thinking individual participants blameworthy in organizational wrongdoing. I turn now to another way that individuals might be thought blameworthy in situations of this kind.

The second source of blameworthiness is a personal failure to distance oneself appropriately from organizational wrongdoing once one becomes aware of it. Clearly, workers at any level of the organizational hierarchy who contribute intentionally to morally dubious collective goals must, by hypothesis, be aware of those goals. This awareness of wrongdoing generates a personal moral reason not to continue participating and not to continue supporting the organizational goals. Recalling the discussion of the difference between collective guilt and personal guilt, particularly with respect to metaphysical guilt, we can see why failure to distance oneself from the collective serves as a basis for individual blameworthiness.

Some might see it as a matter of metaphysical guilt, that is, an issue about who one is or chooses to be; I see it more as a matter of moral guilt, that is, an issue about what one chooses to do and how one understands one's actions. In this case as described, the agent understands her actions as contributing to organizational activities that she knows to be morally questionable. The decision not to disengage from the wrongfully acting collective is an individual moral matter for which one is morally responsible. Understood in this way, we can see that there is plenty of room to hold individuals responsible in collective action without holding them responsible for collective action per se. Given that the intentional structure of organizations yields agency and supports the attribution of collective moral responsibility for the collective wrongdoing as such to the organization, and given that individuals in power are also implicated in collective wrongdoing and responsible for their contributions to it, we can set aside the worry that collective responsibility might cloak or dilute individual responsibility in cases of collective wrongdoing.

Christopher Kutz offers an analysis in which a broader range of individual participants may be considered complicit in collective wrongdoing (and he gives a uniform analysis of the organizational and the goal-oriented context). He maintains that agents "who contribute to collective acts on an on-going basis will fall into the category of intentional participants so long as they see themselves as part of a collective act, and whether or not they favor the collective goal. If so, they are subject to the inclusive ascription of collective acts."[13] The inclusive ascription is that which we ascribe to agents on the basis of agents understanding themselves as acting in the service of a collective goal. They do not have to undertake every single action that is performed toward the goal to understand themselves as acting in the service of "us," not just "me." This self-understanding implicates them in the acts of coparticipants because, according to Kutz's view, intentional participation in collective action is sufficient basis for such implication, regardless of an agent's level of commitment to or even knowledge of the overall aims of the collective. If Kutz is correct, then the first agents I described—the agents who are alienated from the organization's goals, contribute nothing to high-level decisions, and have their own personal reasons for doing the work they do—are inclusive agents in the business of the Red Cross and so are in some degree accountable for its actions and their consequences, not just for their own direct personal role in the collective undertaking. I think it is consistent with Kutz's view that the second agent—the rogue worker who takes matters into her or his own hands and creates havoc—is best assessed for those acts as an individual. This agent is not interested in the "us" factor as she or he sabotages the blood supply, and is not following the protocol for carrying out organizational policy. And finally, Kutz's view implicates the third kind of agent for the collective acts of the organization because they are sufficiently informed to know exactly what kind of policies they are helping to move along.

The kind of responsibility that may be attributed to us as individuals when we act together to bring about a joint goal is inclusive in Kutz's sense because it is understood that we are responsible for a broader range of acts than just our own contributions; we are inclusively responsible for the actions of the collective as such. Kutz explains that, to the extent that we share a goal, "we are properly held accountable for the actions of groups (and of individual group members) in which we participate because these actions represent our own conception of our agency and our project."[14] Our intentional acts reflect what we are willing and wanting to be doing. The basis for an ascription of responsibility here is teleological, not causal.

I take issue with very little of what Kutz has to say. One difference between our views is that Kutz offers a uniform analysis of organizational collective contexts and goal-oriented collective contexts, whereas I distinguish between them. I do so because I think their different intentional structures alter the nature of the relationship between the whole and the individual members who function within it. The primary analytical difference between our views helps to explain why Kutz does not feel the need to draw a distinction. Whereas I believe that agents who exert little or no causal power to determine or bring about organizational goals are not responsible for the actions of the collective agent, Kutz detaches individual responsibility from causal contribution and locates it more squarely in the teleological link to the collective goal that the agent's participatory intention supplies. This is not to say that, on my view, individual agents are not responsible for anything at all. As I argue above, they are responsible both for their contributions and for their failure to disassociate from the organization. I should clarify, of course, that the sense in which Kutz thinks they are responsible is the inclusive sense; they are inclusive, not necessarily exclusive, authors of the collective action. Individuals are exclusive authors and thus exclusively responsible only for what they do themselves. According to my view, only the collective agent as a whole is the exclusive author of a collective action. In an organizational context, at the collective level there are no exclusive authors of collective acts. The notion of inclusive authorship does not, in my view, give us a foothold on which to distinguish who shoulders a greater burden of responsibility. In the organizational context especially, given the formal structures, the role definition, and the way the structures empower individuals such that their acts have more reach than they otherwise would, there are additional responsibility-making factors besides individuals' intentions to participate on which to base attributions of individual responsibility in the collective wrongdoing of organizations. The empowering dimension of the organizational structures plays a key role in grounding individual responsibility in organizational action and in accounting for differences in degree.

Because I maintain that the intentional structures of organizations operate differently from the intentional structures of goal-oriented collectives, I think a different analysis of individual responsibility is warranted for each. Before I move on to individual responsibility in goal-oriented collectives, let me return to the question with which I began this section: in cases of organizational wrongdoing, for what are individuals responsible? My short answer is that they are not responsible for collective actions as such. But it is possible and even likely that some individuals, particularly those in positions of authority, will be implicated to a large degree because their authority, as defined by the organization's formal structures, gives them greater influence over the direction and actions of the organization. Thus, in cases of wrongdoing in organizations, individuals who play major roles in setting the direction and intention of the organization are blameworthy when those directions and intentions yield blameworthy collective behavior, as in the case of the Canadian Red Cross. Individuals in positions of lesser or no authority are more akin to cogs in the organizational machine. Their actions in their roles might be among the constituents of the organization's intentional actions, but these agents do not shape or determine the intentions or interests of the organization. In some cases, their level of commitment to or knowledge of the organization's blameworthy goals will make them blameworthy as well—not, however, for the organizational wrongdoing over which they had little influence but instead for their own contribution and their failure to disassociate. I now turn to individual responsibility in cases of collective wrong in goal-oriented collectives.

4.3 INDIVIDUAL MORAL RESPONSIBILITY IN THE WRONGDOING OF GOAL-ORIENTED COLLECTIVE AGENTS

A goal-oriented collective agent differs from an organizational collective agent insofar as the glue that holds goal-oriented collectives together and gives them their identity is not a formal structure—they do not have one—but rather a joint commitment to a particular goal. In chapter 1 I provided a range of examples, including a group of people doing the wave at a sports event, two people going for a walk together, and the runners in a charity race to raise money for cancer research. There, I maintained as well that the perpetrators of the Rwandan genocide constitute a goal-oriented collective agent, distinguished in kind from an organizational collective agent and from a collective that is not an agent at all. A defining feature of genocide is that it is done with the intent to destroy a group. The genocidal goal with which the perpetrators act together as a group, understanding themselves as engaging in a collective act meant to bring about their goal, supports the interpretation of them as a goal-oriented collective. In this respect, they differ from organizational collective agents and from groups of people whose actions have a cumulative impact that is not intended as a collective goal and not the result of a joint venture. I have suggested that some environmental harms are best understood in the latter way, not as the work of a collective agent. In what follows, I will consider the nature of individual responsibility in the context of a goal-oriented collective's wrongdoing.

As I argued above about individual responsibility in organizational contexts, I argue here that in goal-oriented collectives, individuals are responsible as individuals for their contributions to collective acts, not for collective acts as such. The structure of the intentions of goal-oriented collectives and the manner in which these ground moral responsibility at the collective level account for responsibility for collective acts themselves. Collective agents are morally responsible for intentional collective actions; goal-oriented collectives are one kind of collective agent. Their intentionality admits of degrees—some collective goal-oriented endeavors involve more or less cohesiveness than others. When there is no cohesiveness at all, agency thoroughly falls away and there is merely parallel action at the individual level. Such actions may have harmful results, but if they do not result from collective agency, then where there is moral responsibility it must be at the level of individuals. The main claim I wish to make here is that in cases of intentional collective action undertaken by goal-oriented collectives, individual moral responsibility is not erased or overridden because of facts about collective moral responsibility.

The analysis that follows has an individualist flavor. The reason for this is its scope: it is a discussion of individual moral responsibility in goal-oriented collectives. Responsibility at the individual level does not replace, but rather is additional to, the moral responsibility we might assign to the collective itself for its actions. Given my two-level view of moral responsibility, it will not come as a surprise that I will argue here, as I have with respect to organizational collective contexts, that individuals are responsible for their contributions to collective actions but not for collective actions per se. Once again, it is useful to bear in mind the distinction between individual responsibility for collective action and individual responsibility in collective action. Holding individuals responsible for collective action holds them, as individuals, responsible for actions that are far beyond their reach. As noted earlier, goal-oriented collective actions—whether they are in some sense essentially so, for example dancing a tango, or only so in a particular manifestation,

for example a specific genocide that is jointly pursued—are undertaken by groups of individuals acting together in the service of a
collective goal. Insofar as the actions are collective, no one participant performs the entire act. More than that, no one in these joint
ventures intends or even can intend the entire act. Participants
might share in their commitment to a collective goal but, I have
argued, it is a feature of the collectivity of actions of this kind that
they are the products of collective, not individual, intentions.
What is pertinent for the present discussion is that, nonetheless,
individuals who participate in the actions of goal-oriented collectives contribute because they embrace the goal and understand
themselves as working together with others to achieve it. When
the goal is morally reprehensible, their commitment to the joint
goal, their allegiance to the collective agent who might bring it
about, and the intentional contributions they make to it—
intentional because they make them as contributions to the joint
enterprise—all constitute possible grounds for blameworthiness
in collective action, even if not possible grounds for blameworthiness for collective action, because each of these behaviors makes it
plausible to describe the contribution in a way that highlights its
morally reprehensible qualities.

Let us turn now to the specific example of the Rwandan genocide, not in all of its detail but rather in something of a sketch
meant to highlight the manner in which individuals who participate in goal-oriented collective endeavors are responsible for their
contributions. I should qualify my use of this example by noting
that my reason for using it is to elucidate a moral, not legal, understanding of responsibility in this collectively undertaken atrocity. I
have maintained a number of times that the genocide in Rwanda
qualifies as the action of a goal-oriented collective agent. And
although there were also some organizational elements involved,

the extent of participation went far beyond organized militia and Rwandan military—upward of one hundred thousand Rwandans, including many ordinary citizens, contributed to the slaughter of close to one million Tutsi and Tutsi sympathizers in April 1994, with the explicit goal of destroying the Tutsi population completely. The reason for my claim that it involved collective agency is not the simple fact that there were many perpetrators. It is, of course, possible, that many people could act in a parallel instead of collective fashion with the same result. However, the claim that the participants in the Rwandan genocide acted with this genocidal goal in mind is neither controversial nor contested. The goal, given the size of the population at whose destruction they aimed and the reality that in this case the end could not be achieved alone, was a joint goal. And the individuals understood themselves as acting together with others to achieve it. Thus, given my view that goal-oriented collective agents form when individuals coalesce around a joint goal and see themselves as acting together with others to bring it about, the perpetrators of the Rwandan genocide constitute a goal-oriented collective agent under the terms of my account.

The most often-cited worry about claiming that individual contributors are responsible only for their respective parts is that in a case like this one, in which no one individual is responsible for the death of all of the victims, no one appears to be morally responsible for the genocide as a whole. Yet the atrocity of genocide is clearly morally reprehensible and something for which we would like to be able to hold an agent blameworthy. Seumas Miller puts the concern this way: "naturally, each member is individually responsible for his or her individual acts of murder, or for assisting in the murder of a given person, or for planning an attack, or for whatever contributory action he or she performed. But how do we escape the conclusion that no one is morally responsible for the genocide as such?"[15]

My analysis escapes this undesirable conclusion by attributing responsibility for the genocide as such to the goal-oriented collective agent. But it also takes us beyond the kinds of descriptions Miller suggests for the individual contributions. He speaks of responsibility for murders or assisting in murder or in planning attacks. But the theory of act descriptions invoked earlier in this chapter suggests a more comprehensive—in Williams's terms, "thicker"—description that carries with it the particular and unique moral weight of genocide. We do not trivialize murder by claiming that these are not simple acts of murder. Instead, when we describe them as contributions to genocide, performed intentionally as contributions to genocide, that is, with the aim of destroying a group—in this particular case an aim understood as being jointly pursued—their moral character changes. In fact, in the context of international law, many of these acts could qualify as acts of genocide. That they might so qualify does not, however, provide the answer we are seeking to Miller's question. For that question presses us to find an agent responsible for the collective atrocity: the genocide as such. Furthermore, as Miller's statement of his question shows, there is a strong sense in which the "popular" understanding of genocide is as the mass atrocity, not as this or that perpetrator's contributions to it. When we redescribe a murder as "a contribution to genocide," there is no question that this redescription highlights a particular, telling, and blameworthy feature of the act's moral character. This harkens back to the accordion effect and the way it can reveal more or less about an action's character and consequences. Sometimes the information will have moral import, sometimes it will not. The information that an act is a contribution to genocide, given that genocide presupposes a malicious intent with specific content, provides us with important information for moral evaluation and for the assignment of blameworthy responsibility. And it does that without having to go the further step of inferring that a given individual is morally responsible for the genocide as a whole.

I examined Kutz's analysis in my discussion of organizational collective agents. It is even more to the point with respect to goal-oriented collective agents, because Kutz does not draw a distinction between these and organizational collective agents. He consciously pursues a minimalist approach that does not depend on elaborate formal structures. His reason for doing so is that he wants an analysis with as broad an application as possible.

As we saw above, Kutz believes that collective wrongs can be proper objects of individual responsibility, and participatory intentions provide the link by serving as the basis for responsibility. The basis is the ground for an ascription of responsibility. Kutz distinguishes between the basis for responsibility and the object of responsibility. The object is that for which an agent is responsible. In the cases under discussion, the object of responsibility is collective, and according to his analysis the individuals, regardless of the scope of their causal contribution, are responsible as individuals for the collective wrong insofar as they act with a participatory intention to contribute to the achievement of the joint goal. The basis on which they are responsible, the participatory intention, is individualistic, not collective. This individualistic basis grounds individual responsibility for the acts of others, namely, for the collective outcome or action. In this way, individuals can be considered responsible for collective wrongs irrespective of the actual causal contribution they make as individuals.[16]

As we have seen, in addition to maintaining that individuals can be responsible for collective wrongs in which they participate, but to which they made no essential difference, Kutz distinguishes between inclusive and exclusive authorship. The two kinds of authorship support the respective ascriptions of inclusive and exclusive responsibility.

It follows from this view that where collective actions are concerned, there is no exclusive author, only a number of inclusive authors whose intention to participate implicates them in responsibility (of the inclusive kind) for the collective act in its entirety. Here is where my view and Kutz's diverge. According to my two-level account of responsibility, the goal-oriented agent is, using Kutz's language, the exclusive author of its collective acts. As such, there is nothing counterintuitive about ascribing responsibility for those acts to it as a collective agent. Because my view accounts for responsibility for the collective act in this manner, I am less drawn to the idea that inclusive authorship grounds a sufficiently meaningful form of agency to support an attribution of responsibility to an individual for a goal-oriented collective's acts in their entirety. Instead, I advocate the view that these individuals are responsible for their parts in bringing about the collective action. That is the essential difference between my view and Kutz's view. Where he believes participatory intentions are the basis for attributions of individual responsibility for collective objects, I do not.

The challenge for a view such as mine is to explain why minimal contributions with little causal impact in the collective act as a whole pose a moral problem and on what basis they are blameworthy or reprehensible. In isolation, individual contributions to collective actions might seem to be morally neutral or close to it, so negligible might be their impact. If that is true, then individuals seem to escape blame even when our intuitions tell us they should not.

I address this concern when I maintain, as I did earlier, that although inclusive authorship is not sufficient to implicate someone as responsible for "the whole thing," it lends shape to our analysis of persons' actions in the context of the whole thing and of their self-understandings of what they are doing. When an agent intentionally acts in relation to a shared goal and her action takes place in the context of the acts of a goal-oriented collective, the breadth of descriptions that we may accurately apply to her act expands to make reference to the collective act. We saw this earlier in the discussion of genocide. An individual's act takes on a unique moral character when it may be described as "a contribution to genocide." Rather than invoking Kutz's idea of inclusive responsibility, I suggest instead that when accurate descriptions of individuals' contributions to the collective actions of goal-oriented collectives reflect the moral character of the collective acts of which they are parts, the acts inherit the moral quality of the whole. Individuals may, therefore, be considered responsible for their contributions, and their contributions receive their moral due when we highlight their intentional connection to the larger plan.

I have provided very little in the way of strong reasons to reject Kutz's analysis on this one point. Instead, I maintain that in the overall context of my two-level theory, inclusive responsibility is not the best way to analyze individuals' contributions to the morally reprehensible actions of goal-oriented collectives. Rather than holding individuals responsible for collective actions, my view attributes collective responsibility to the collective agent, attributes individual responsibility for contributions to collective actions to individual agents who participate, and explains at the same time why, even when these individual contributions make a negligible overall difference, they inherit the moral qualities of the blameworthy whole. For this reason, they are themselves blameworthy contributions, and the agents who perform them are blameworthy in, if not for, the actions of the goal-oriented collective agent.

4.4 CONCLUSION

Throughout the earlier chapters, I maintained that collective moral responsibility does not distribute among individuals who are members of morally responsible collectives. At the same time, I claimed that the nondistributive nature of collective moral responsibility does not preclude moral responsibility at the individual level. An account that implicated collectives by exonerating all individuals engaged in collective ventures would be deficient. According to my view, whether the offending collective agent is an organization or a goal-oriented collective, individuals who play a part in the collective wrongdoing are responsible for their contributions. Depending what sort of agent the offending collective agent is—organizational or goal-oriented—the basis for individual implication will vary. In neither case, however, does a judgment of collective moral responsibility in any way undermine what we may say about individual moral responsibility. This outcome is as it should be, given the two-level understanding of moral responsibility. Collective agents fulfill their own conditions for agency and moral responsibility; individual agents fulfill theirs. And while participation in collective action contexts influences the normative range of what individuals may be responsible for, it does not make them responsible for the acts of collective agents as such.

In the following two chapters I continue my discussion of individual moral responsibility in collective contexts by addressing two further issues. First, I discuss the nature of individual obligation in collective contexts where there is no collective agency—the context of global warming, for example. Second, I take up the issue of the extent to which individuals may be implicated for their participation in wrongful social practice where such practice is widespread and its wrongness is a moral fact about which people are generally ignorant—contexts of oppression, for example. These two discussions depart somewhat from the context of collective moral agency to account for individual responsibility in cases where no obvious collective moral agency exists—there is neither an organization nor a goal-oriented collective acting intentionally in a blameworthy fashion. Yet people are engaged in behavior that, together with the actions of others, has at least a cumulative harmful impact and might even be morally wrong, as in the case of participation in oppression.

I turn first to individual obligation in collective contexts.

[5]

COLLECTIVE OBLIGATION, INDIVIDUAL OBLIGATION, AND INDIVIDUAL MORAL RESPONSIBILITY

Up to now, the majority of my discussion has focused on moral responsibility, both collective and individual, in the context of the actions of organizations and of goal-oriented collectives. In addition, my attention has been on responsibility in the evaluative and predominantly backward-looking sense of praiseworthiness and blameworthiness. I have aimed to articulate the conditions under which collective agents and individual agents may be held responsible for and in collective action situations. In this chapter, I turn my attention to a more forward-looking relative of responsibility, namely, obligation. I do this because after-the-fact assessments of moral praise or blame, important though they may be, are only part of the story. As moral agents, most of us are concerned to know ahead of time what morality requires of us so that we may avoid doing the wrong thing, aim at doing the right thing, and thereby avoid acting in a blameworthy manner and aim at acting in a praiseworthy manner. Of the four examples I outline at the very outset of the book, I claim that two—participation in oppressive social practice and humanity's cumulative impact on the planet in the form of global warming and environmental degradation more generally—are not the work of collective agents. Yet still, no individual on her or his own can even begin to address massive problems of this kind: the only workable solutions to them are collective solutions. My goal in this chapter is to outline a way of thinking about problems of this kind that allows individuals to see their way to action. Even if they are the result of the cumulative impact of human behavior, these harms are not the products of collective action. Nonetheless, they require collective solutions. I argue that the daunting task for individuals of knowing what their part as individuals is in ameliorating these seemingly insurmountable harms is made easier when we invoke the idea of a collective obligation. The collective obligation can play a mediating role, providing some shape and order to the range of individual actions; it helps to narrow down the field of possible individual actions, making it more manageable. The challenge, however, is that these are exactly the cases in which I have denied that a collective agent—either organization or goal-oriented collective—is morally responsible at the collective level. Thus, a significant part of the project of this chapter is to motivate the possibility of thinking in terms of collective obligation in the absence of an organization or a goal-oriented collective. I do not begin with this challenge. Instead, I begin with comparatively clearer cases—organizations and goal-oriented collectives—to demonstrate what I mean by the claim that collective obligation performs a mediating role with respect to individual obligation in collective action scenarios.

5.1 ORGANIZATIONAL OBLIGATION, INDIVIDUAL OBLIGATION, AND INDIVIDUAL RESPONSIBILITY

Just as collective action is the action of a collective agent and collective moral responsibility is the moral responsibility of a collective agent, so collective obligation is the obligation of a collective agent.

Once we countenance the existence of collective agents and allow that there is collective moral responsibility, we have no reason to deny collective obligation. Understood in the terms of the two-level account I have developed and argued for so far, collective obligation operates at a level distinct from individual obligation. In order to discharge its obligations at the collective level, a collective agent requires that its members fulfill their functions. The duties associated with roles within a collective will be in large part determined by, though they are distinct from, the obligations of the collective as a whole.

In the case of organizations, it is relatively easy to determine collective obligations. As long as we remain at the collective level of discussion, complications are few. Governments have an obligation to serve their citizens; corporations have an obligation to treat their employees fairly; universities have an obligation to serve their students' educational needs; and so on. These collective entities—organizations—have structures and decision procedures in place, as well as defined roles and hierarchies, that give them identities that are independent of the particular individuals who are their members at a given time. Their obligations are also independent of their members. For example Nike Corporation has an obligation to treat its workers fairly regardless of who the executive officers or the rank and file employees are. The collective obligation transcends the identities of individuals. More generally, organizations have moral obligations to conduct their operations in a morally acceptable manner. Somewhat more challenging than the task of articulating the obligations of organizations is the task of articulating the relationship between these and the relevantly related obligations of particular individuals within the organization.

The most straightforward approach is to claim that individuals are required to fulfill the responsibilities of their respective roles within the organization. One of the features of an organization is the structure, which coordinates the machinations of the collective agent. As we have seen, the structure outlines the roles that individuals are meant to play, that is, what their jobs are. For example, a university has an obligation to pay its employees. In keeping with the two-level account of agency, then, we can see that it is a collective obligation because its subject is a collective agent. There is no one individual member of the university whose personal obligation it is to pay the employees. If we claim that collective obligations shape individual obligations, in that they help to define the roles of individuals within the organization, then paying the employees will be in the purview of the people in the payroll office. To the extent that they perform the duties associated with their respective roles, they are doing their part in relation to the collective obligation. According to this proposal, collective obligations dictate the requirements of individuals' roles, and the individuals' obligations in the organizational context are exhausted by the requirements of their roles. The view has a number of difficulties, to which I now turn.

The first difficulty concerns the nature of the various roles within an organized collective. In very large organizations, some jobs are more well-defined than others. For example, the expectations and tasks of the clerk in payroll or the data-entry person in the programming room are all typically laid out in the job description. If someone calls in sick and a temporary replacement comes in, the replacement does exactly the same thing as the person she or he is replacing. Contrast this with the roles of faculty members, department chairs, deans, and the president within the university structure. There is a lot of room for variation in how the occupants of these roles discharge the associated duties. Although some of the tasks—for example, a faculty member's teaching responsibilities or a dean's responsibility to balance the budget—are clear, others, for example a faculty member's research commitments and a dean's efforts at fundraising or contributions to recruitment and retention, are less clear. The more responsibility one has within the collective, the less obvious the specifics are of what one is required to do and how one is required to do it. Moreover, the roles in which it is less clear and there is more latitude are precisely the roles that are likely to be most directly responsive to the collective's obligations. Those in power are in a better position to ensure that the collective acts as it ought. This point is very like the claim in the previous chapter that those in positions of power in an organization carry a heavier burden of responsibility as individuals because the structures of the organization expand the range of their powers as individuals. We see a notable asymmetry between the more powerful and less powerful roles within an organized collective. To the extent that the manner in which one is to carry out one's role is less defined and as one's power increases, the scope of personal choice within the role also increases. This increase in latitude at the level of personal choice lends further weight to the claim, defended in chapter 4, that persons in positions of power ought to be considered more responsible than those who work in the mailroom when an organization fulfills or fails to fulfill its obligations. In the context of collective obligation, individuals' obligations intensify when they have more power and more room for personal choice with respect to how they fulfill their roles. Collective actions require the actions of individuals, and certain individuals are in a better position than others to direct the actions of the collective and to see that the collective's intentional actions are consistent with its obligations as a collective. This is not to say that people in positions of lesser power cannot interfere in significant ways with the fulfillment of collective obligations. Certainly, someone in the payroll office can wreak havoc.[1] But the nature of their duties is clear, so deviations from them are also clear.

While some people have worried that collective agency trivializes individual agency by subsuming it,[2] this discussion reiterates the claim that, on the contrary, rather than disappearing against the background of collective obligation, individual obligation can take on a heightened importance. The reason is that a collective context empowers and authorizes some individuals so that they can achieve outcomes that they could not otherwise achieve. For example, in the role of president of a university, an agent is able to make decisions that she or he would not be able to make were she or he not in that role. A president can close departments, shut down programs, define a university's place in the broader community, and sometimes even overrule decisions made by other governing bodies within the university. These obligations of the president in the presidential role, while less specific with respect to the exact form that carrying them out will take, are more closely and directly related to the obligations of the collective than the obligations of the payroll clerk, whose role is spelled out with more precision concerning specific tasks, with less room for personal choice within it. The upshot of this discussion is that the suggestion that in an organized collective the relationship between collective obligation and individual obligation is fully captured by the specification of roles falters when we consider that in more powerful roles, the form of the individuals' duties in the role is less specified and there is much room for personal choice.

Roles fall short in fully capturing the relationship between collective and individual obligation in an organization for a further reason: regardless of how well-defined someone's role within an organization is, the dictates of the role do not exhaust what is required of individuals with respect to meeting the organization's collective moral obligations. Consider, for example, the moral inadequacy of the Nazi concentration camp workers' claims that they were "just doing their jobs." Within the context of their roles, they may have been doing exactly what was expected of them. However, the collective within which they were functioning in their roles was not just failing to meet its collective moral obligations, it was positively violating them in a way that even relatively powerless participants could reasonably be expected to know. When a collective has obligations that are not being met, this failure shapes and alters the obligations of individual members as members of the collective. Someone might question the idea that the collective obligation in this kind of case mediates the individual obligation in any way; perhaps it is more accurate to claim that the individuals in the Nazi case are violating obligations as individuals, simpliciter.[3] Two points are worth noting here. First, recall that we are discussing difficulties facing the claim that role-related duties exhaust the range of individual obligations in organized collectives. The claim under discussion is that there is reason to think that they do not. Second, even if an individual's actions would be wrong outside the collective context, the collective context in which they take place increases the range of morally relevant descriptions that apply to an individual's action. Individual actions taken in the Holocaust as contributions to the collective action of genocide have an added moral dimension that is not captured without reference to the collective action. The further dimension adds gravity to the contributions individuals make.

In whistle-blowing cases, we see a similar shortcoming of the view that individual obligation in organizations is exhausted by roles. In these cases, the collective's failure to fulfill its collective obligations creates a scenario in which individuals, as moral agents, are morally required to do something that goes beyond their usual duties in order to "help" the collective fulfill its obligations. Once again, we see that claiming that individuals' obligations within a collective are defined only by their roles is not enough to account for circumstances of collective moral failure. When the collective is acting as it ought, individuals who are performing their role-related duties as specified by their job descriptions are doing their part in making sure that the collective meets its moral obligations. Further action is required only when something goes wrong. This may lead some to say that whistle-blowing, or doing anything that takes one beyond the dictates of one's role to ensure that collective moral obligations are fulfilled, is supererogatory. That is, some might claim that actions of this kind are morally laudable, but not required, because they go beyond moral obligation and enter into the realm of the heroic. One reason for not making this claim is that by continuing to do one's job in conditions of collective moral failing, one knowingly contributes to morally wrongful collective action. These contributions themselves are morally wrong. It is morally required, not supererogatory, to cease acting in a morally wrong way. Thus, we may conclude that collective moral obligations sometimes alter the obligations of individual members of organizations beyond the dictates of the members' organizational roles.

Despite the individuals' duties in their roles not being exhaustive of the moral obligations they may face in those roles, organizations provide the most straightforward illustration of the way collective obligations can influence and constrain the obligations of individuals. An organization's actions typically flow from a system of well-articulated decision procedures. As a result, there are systems in place that make it easier to meet collective obligations. Moreover, the existence of a decision procedure helps to define the collective, and thus to ground the existence of collective obligations. Let us briefly turn our attention to the moral obligations of goal-oriented collectives before moving on to cases that require a collective action solution but lack an obvious collective agent whose obligation it is to carry out that solution.

Goal-oriented collectives are less structured than organizations. But they, too, are moral agents, subject to praise and blame, and they, too, can have moral obligations. Some of these obligations might be directly related to the goal; others might be more general. For example, the goal-oriented collective whose goal is to destroy a population group because of its ethnicity in fact has a moral obligation collectively not to pursue that goal. Collective agents are as bound by moral principles as human agents are. Violating these principles leaves the agents subject to blame. Moreover, these collective obligations in turn shape the individual moral requirements of the collective's members. For example, agents who are acting as members of goal-oriented collectives are constrained at the individual level not to contribute to morally reprehensible collective goals.

It might seem obvious and facile to say that individuals, qua individuals, are obligated not to participate in morally reprehensible collective goals. My specific claim is that the individual obligation is significantly mediated by the collective obligation not to engage in the collective wrongdoing. This points us back to the earlier discussion about the moral qualities that individual behavior inherits when it is undertaken as part of a collective endeavor. Individuals' actions in these collective undertakings do not have the moral character they have in the absence of the larger collective scheme of which they are a part. The obligations of the collective do not distribute to individuals, but they do constrain the obligations of individuals, suggesting particular courses of actions individuals may permissibly take (or are not permitted to take) in the service of the collective ends.

This point holds similarly for laudable goals. If a goal-oriented collective is formed around a morally laudable goal—perhaps the goal of raising money for cancer research by holding an annual race—the collective aim helps to shape the way individuals may play a part. For example, in the absence of this goal-oriented collective, the task of tackling the disease of cancer (in general, not a specific instantiation of it in someone) on my own is daunting. I would not know where to start. But in the context of this larger fundraising effort, my options begin to take shape: if I want to participate but am not a runner, then I might sponsor someone instead; if I like to run, then it makes sense for me to take part in the race and ask other people to sponsor me. It is not simply the case that my small part gains significance because it is part of a collective effort that raises $20 million for cancer research. There is the further point that the collective framework itself helps narrow down my range of options, thus enabling me to take effective action against a daunting and individually insoluble problem.

5.2 MAPPING AND CLARITY

The collective agency contexts discussed in the previous section demonstrate the way collective obligations and collective goals can shape and influence the obligations of individuals. The moral features of collective agents, therefore, play a mediating role with respect to the obligations of individuals who contribute to the collective's actions. The most challenging cases are those in which there is no organization or goal-oriented collective, yet a coordinated effort appears to be required to alleviate the harm or suffering in question. These cases occupy the murky middle ground between collective and individual obligation. They are difficult to capture in terms of collective agency because it is not clear who the collective agent might be. At the same time, however, to stay at the level of individual obligation and responsibility risks taking a view that is too narrow, in the sense that it does not adequately appreciate that a collective action solution is going to be far more effective than an individual action solution.[4] Indeed, issues of global poverty, world hunger and disease, and environmental destruction appear so immense from the perspective of the individual that no action within the reach of ordinary moral agents seems likely to make much of a difference. The amount of actual and potential human suffering in these kinds of situations is enormous. As a result, it is difficult not to view them as moral issues. We face a great challenge in attempting to chart the territory of individual obligation in the context of moral issues that are so large that they require collective action solutions. It is tempting to think that the need for a collective action solution suggests that we are in fact dealing with a collective moral obligation that directs and grounds the obligations of individuals. Invoking the sort of model proposed above would then be helpful. But the idea of a collective obligation without a collective agent who is so obligated appears to be a stretch. The rest of this chapter is an attempt to argue that when collective action solutions come into focus and potential collective agents with relatively clear identities emerge as the subjects of those actions, then we may understand individual obligations as we did above, namely, as flowing from collective obligations that those potential agents would have.

The arrest and repair of environmental degradation, responding to the dangers of global warming, famine relief and global poverty, emergency aid and assistance in rebuilding after natural disasters—these all require mobilization at the collective level. The scale of the problems mandates large-scale solutions. Collective solutions map easily onto challenges of this kind. Individual solutions fall short, not just because they are akin to attempting to put out a blazing house with a toy water pistol but also because the scale of the issues makes it difficult for an individual to know where to begin to address them. We saw this in the cancer research example. From the standpoint of the individual, these problems are insurmountable. Yet from the standpoint of collective action, we might be able to tackle them. What is needed to address these challenges successfully is for individuals to see themselves as playing a part in collective action solutions. At the level of collective action, there is more clarity concerning what might help.

It is worth pausing over this point about clarity at the collective level and my claim that collective solutions "map" easily, or at least more easily, onto these large problems than individual solutions do. In order to explain what I mean, let me turn to a series of examples in which it becomes increasingly difficult to see what the situation demands and of whom. I'll call these Bystander Cases, even though we may recognize the limits of that idea when we reflect on certain cases, such as global warming, in which some may claim that no one is actually a mere bystander; all are participants. In a Bystander Case, there is at least one person suffering a harm and at least one person in a position to assist. The person or persons in a position to assist is or are not backwardly responsible for the plight of those in need, so the obligation to assist, if there is one, does not turn on any prior share in bringing the unfortunate circumstances about. Imagine:

> Bystander Case 1: You are reading a book on a riverbank. You glance up from your book and see a child drowning very nearby. No one else is around, and you are a proficient swimmer trained in lifesaving techniques. You can easily rescue the child with only a minor inconvenience to yourself.

Commonsense morality and most normative moral theories dictate that, other things being equal, you have a moral obligation to make your best attempt to rescue the child. In cases such as these when there is just one victim, one bystander equipped to help, and a clear course of action that would help, we see a straightforward mapping of obligation to situation. Now consider:

> Bystander Case 2: You are reading a book on a riverbank. You glance up from your book and see two children drowning. Both are near you, but they are not very close to each other. No one else is around, and you are a proficient swimmer trained in life saving techniques. You can easily rescue either child with only a minor inconvenience to yourself, but, given their locations in the water, you are not likely to be able to rescue both.

Most moral theories claim that, other things being equal, you have a moral obligation to make your best attempt to rescue one of the children even if you cannot rescue both. As we can see from this example, the mapping between obligation and circumstance is less exact, the course of action less clear—two alternatives present themselves. But some clarity remains: if you fail to take any action, you will have failed morally. You must take one of two options.

In each of the above cases, there is only one bystander. When there are more than one, there is no direct mapping of a particular individual's obligation onto the situation. These situations can take different forms, some of which are more collective than others. First, there are situations in which someone is suffering a harm and there is more than one person in a position to assist, though only one person's assistance is needed. The first riverbank scenario above would be like this if there were several people at the riverside who could save the drowning child. Second, there are situations in which more than one person is suffering a harm, and more than one person is in a position to assist. The second riverbank case would be like this if there was at least one other person in a position to assist.

Alternatively, there might be multiple people in need and multiple people available to assist, but perhaps not enough to save everyone.

Consider the first kind of case in which one person needs assistance, only one assistant is required, and more than one person is available to help. Though it involves more than one bystander, this case does not demand collective action. As described, only one individual is needed to assist, making it a case of an individual obligation that a number of different people could fulfill. Individual obligation maps neatly onto the situation for each, but only conditionally so. The presence of other potential rescuers affects the obligation of each by making it conditional; if another bystander fulfills the moral obligation to save the drowning child, the others are no longer required to act. However, if no one steps forward to save the child, and the child ends up drowning, then each fails to meet an individual moral obligation. As long as the condition is not met, each person's moral obligation is unambiguous: rescue the drowning child unless someone else does.

Consider now a case that requires collective action:

Coordinated Bystander Case: Four bystanders are relaxing on the riverbank when six children on a raft run into trouble when they and their raft end up in rapids. They are hurtling helplessly toward a dangerous waterfall downriver and are unlikely to survive if they go over it. Nothing any of the four bystanders can do as an individual will make a difference, but there is an obvious course of coordinated action they could take to divert the raft into calmer waters. This measure would pose little risk to the bystanders and would save all of the children.

Here, at the collective level, there is a clear map between the situation, the required course of action and a collective agent. The collective agent who would save the day has not, however, been formed. It may be obvious who the members should be, but they have not yet come together as a collective. The idea of potential collective agents warrants our attention, and I turn to that next. But first, let me restate my point that though as individuals, the bystanders in this last case cannot see a solution, the collective solution is clear. Global warming, poverty, hunger—these global challenges mirror this kind of bystander case. As we've seen, the range of possible actions one might take as an individual is daunting, and in the end none appears to have potential to make a difference. However, from a collective point of view, the map reads more clearly. For example, if collectively we want to reduce carbon emissions in order to slow or stop global warming, then we must change our collective behavior. Collectively, there are solutions. Moreover, these collective solutions— particularly if they can be understood as collective obligations of sorts—can help to define and narrow down the range of contributions individual participants might take. The trouble is, of course, that the referent of the "we" is not obvious, and furthermore it remains unclear how this solution that we (collectively) could engage in might involve me (individually).

5.3 RANDOM COLLECTIONS AND PUTATIVE GROUPS

Random collections of people, for example the bystanders beside the river, the audience at an orchestral performance, the lunch crowd at the diner last Friday, are not unified by anything beyond happenstance. Peter French has noted of these kinds of collections that "although there may be exceptions, members usually are together in that place at that time because of each individual's pursuit of his own ends."[5] But some slight change in circumstance, for example the plight of the children on the raft, can create the conditions under which a random group reconfigures itself into a goal-oriented collective capable of intentional action as a collective. The individuals on the beach can come together with the purpose of saving the children. When a random collection does not spring into action to form itself into a goal-oriented collective or an organization, then it is what Larry May calls a "putative group," and its failure is a case of collective inaction.[6] When existing collective agents decide not to act in circumstances that demand action, their failures are collective omissions, outcomes of decision procedures. The idea of a putative group suggests that there may be room to establish collective obligation in the absence of collective agency—potential collective agency may provide grounds for collective obligation, either actual or also putative obligation, following May's terminology. If so, then, as I shall claim, those obligations might have the same mediating effect that they do in cases of actual collective agency, insofar as they can shape and order individuals' roles.

May claims that where putative groups fail to act, we can hold them responsible for failure to organize as a group that could take action. That means they fail to develop a decision procedure or a sense of solidarity (what I have been thinking of in terms of coalescing around a particular goal) that would enable them collectively to act. I find this idea attractive because it gives some support to the possibility of collective obligation in the absence of an existing collective agent, and this, in turn, helps to shed light on moral possibilities for individuals who might see themselves becoming more effective agents when they join forces with others. Though the idea is attractive, the nature of the failure warrants further attention.

David Copp challenges the notion of holding putative groups responsible for failing to organize, on the grounds that developing the characteristics that make a group capable of collective action—for example decision procedures, a sense of solidarity, shared goals—is itself a collective action. If putative groups can develop these features without having them already, then it's not clear to Copp why we should suppose that these are essential features of collective agency at all.[7] I agree with Copp that there is something paradoxical in the idea of the development of collective agency. But the argument points to an infinite regress that commonsense tells us does not obtain. Where the argument missteps is in the assumption that the same features required for collective action are required for a group to develop into a collective agent. But even if we cannot always point to the exact moment when a collection of people becomes a collective agent, we know that transformations of this kind take place all the time. Take a simple case: nothing binds you and me together as a collective agent; but when we decide to go for a walk together, we become a goal-oriented collective. And recall the example of attendees at a sports event doing the wave. The wave is an excellent example of a collective action—its success requires that people intentionally participate together with others in the service of a common goal: to produce the wave effect throughout the stands, rolling neatly and predictably from one section to the next and continuing around until it peters out. No decision procedure is settled in advance, and no sense of solidarity or shared goal, at least with respect to wave production—exists at the outset. The collective goal arises through the persistence of a small group of people in one section whose enthusiasm catches on and draws others in to the collective effort. Successful waves abound. And so do unsuccessful attempts. It is clearly the case that for any typical sports audience, they could develop the enthusiasm to participate in a wave even if in a given instance they do not. If the capacity is there, then it seems correct to claim, at a minimum, that they failed to organize. Whether that failure constitutes a moral failure is, of course, a separate question that will turn on what they failed to do. But that it constitutes a failure of sorts is a reasonable claim. We might still ask, however, whether the failure is collective or individual. According to my view of collective agency, we need to see this as a failure of individuals because it takes place in the absence of a collective agent. Nonetheless, in situations involving significant moral stakes, the obligations connected to putative groups have an important impact on the obligations of individuals to organize. I explain this claim in what follows.

Virginia Held also wonders about an infinite regress: "Can there be responsibility for not deciding upon a method to decide upon a method to decide upon a method . . . to act?"[8] She responds to this concern by noting that different contexts require the adoption of different decision methods, ranging from allowing the most knowledgeable to decide to consensus, to a majority vote, to the more minimalist sort of implicit understanding required for a successful wave. As we have seen, the same features that may allow a group to organize itself as a group may not be sufficient or appropriate for effective mobilization in response to a situation requiring collective action. Held is right to note this variance. Once a random collection becomes an effective agent, it is no longer a random collection—it is either an organization or a goal-oriented collective. There may be grey moments during which it is not clear what stage of transformation a given collection is at, but not to note a difference between random collections and collective agents would trivialize the idea of agency.

Held goes further than May because she believes not only that a random collection of persons—a putative group—can be considered responsible for not organizing, but that such potential collective agents can be held responsible for failing to take the required course of action. This further step strongly suggests the presence of collective obligation in some cases where a group is neither an organization nor a goal-oriented collective but instead putative. Held invokes the idea of the reasonable person test to determine when this is appropriate: it is appropriate when the "action called for in a given situation is obvious to the reasonable person and when the expected outcome of the action is clearly favorable."[9] If, by contrast, "the action called for is not obvious to the reasonable person a random collection may not be held responsible for not performing the action in question, but, in some cases, may be held responsible for not forming itself into an organized group capable of deciding which action to take."[10] The main feature of Held's view that I want to pick up on here is the idea that the course of action required of a random collection could, in some cases, be clear, at least to the reasonable person. According to Held, when it is clear, then there is an obligation at the collective level for which the collective, putative though it may be, will be responsible if it does not fulfill it. The group as a group, not just the individuals as individuals, is responsible for its failure to take action. In cases such as these, argues Held, the responsibility of the group distributes among all of its members as well, because they failed as individuals to engage in the requisite action for organizing into an effective agent and fulfilling the collective obligation. This analysis of the case suggests that the failure is at two levels. First, there is a failure to meet a collective obligation, and second, given the clarity of that obligation, there is a failure in each individual to join together with the others. The collective obligation exists in virtue of the clarity, by the standard of the reasonable person, of the collective action required. Where there is a lack of clarity at the collective level, what is lacking is a clear picture of what collective courses of action would effectively address the moral concern. I hesitate to attribute actual obligations to potential agents, but as I explain in what follows, a minor adjustment to Held's analysis will address this concern.

My goal in this section is to show how, even in the case of potential collective agents, collective obligations can help to yield more determinate moral requirements for individuals who are members of the collectives. Instead of claiming that putative groups can have actual obligations, I maintain that when the clarity condition is met concerning the required course of collective action, the putative group has a putative obligation. I believe further, however, that when the clarity condition is met with respect to the putative collective obligation, it has exactly the same ordering and mediating potential for individual action that an actual collective obligation would. In either case, it is a mechanism through which individual moral possibility becomes clearer. Thus, my modification of Held's view does not in any way undermine the merits of her point and, more important for my present goals, does not compromise its aptness for supporting my more general claim concerning the relationship between collective obligation and individual obligation in the absence of actual collective agents.

Clarity at the collective level does not always translate into equal clarity at the individual level. However, once it is clear what is required of the collective, the collective obligation has a derivative impact on the obligations of individuals. Members are, in virtue of their position in a collective with an obligation to act, required to sort out appropriate roles and tasks such that the collective action can take place. The presence of even a putative collective obligation, therefore, begins to impose some order on the actions and obligations of individuals acting in the service of a collective end. To the extent that a means for achieving the end is in reach, the putative collective obligation grounds actual obligations for individuals. When there is no clear putative collective obligation in sight, then there is no mechanism for morally requiring that individuals coordinate their actions in a manner that would address the issue at hand. Not every unacceptable situation has—though it may at some point come to have—a clear moral solution, collective or otherwise.

In addition to lending shape to the obligations of individuals, the perspective of the collective obligation, even when putative, furnishes a further normative advantage. For in giving shape to the individual obligations, collective obligation provides a framework for understanding the moral dimensions of individual contributions and individual failures. This point is an extension of the claim, developed earlier, that collective moral responsibility is necessary for an adequate understanding of individual responsibility in collective contexts. Whether the individual contributes to collective action or collective inaction, the moral features of the individual's contribution become salient only against the background of the moral features of the collective action or inaction. For example, although one individual taking a completely individualistic view of a large moral issue such as global warming could abdicate responsibility as an individual by noting that she cannot make a difference, her failure to contribute to a collective effort that would make a difference is not so easily excused. Mediated by a putative collective obligation in which she could participate, her failing is not that she did not solve the problem of global warming—that is something we could never expect her to do. Instead, her failure is that she did not do her part in a collective action that could solve global warming. Because a clear collective action to address this issue is possible and evident to the reasonable person, a putative collective obligation exists. More important, this putative collective obligation, as much as an actual collective obligation would be, is a starting point for bridging the apparent gap between seemingly inconsequential individual contributions and new understandings of the part they play in more powerful collective undertakings. To take us back the puzzle that preceded this section, they allow individuals to begin to see how a solution that we (collectively) could engage in can involve me (as an individual). They expand our moral options by providing a foothold for seeing what is possible. In this manner, they work on our moral imaginations, not in a fanciful way but in ways that point to achievable possibilities.

I have been arguing that we should follow May and Held in thinking that we should give some attention to the moral obligations of collections of people that could, if they organized, become effective as goal-oriented collectives or organizations. These putative collective agents can, when they meet the normative standard of being clear to the reasonable person, have putative collective obligations. Putative collective obligations perform the same function as actual collective obligations with respect to the role they play as mechanisms for making more determinate the possible actions individuals may take as participants in collective endeavors. In what follows, I consider a number of objections to this proposal.

First, some might question whether in the absence of a decision procedure, organizational structure, sense of solidarity, or shared goal a putative collective can be the subject of a moral obligation, even a putative one, that has a binding effect on potential individual members. Obligation seems appropriate only to agents, and these putative groups are, by hypothesis, not quite agents. If we allow that potential collective agents have obligations, then perhaps any mereological sum of agents has the potential to make a difference and so would have a putative collective obligation that governs the obligations of individuals who might become members of the organization or goal-oriented collective, should it materialize. According to this objection, my view might be too broad because any conceivable collective action could be required of any conceivable collection of individuals. For example, there is likely some value-promoting action that the Queen of England, the colleague in the south-facing unit on the second floor, and my third-grade teacher could do together. Does this mean that this putative group has a putative collective obligation to form itself into a group and take action? In order to respond to this concern, it is necessary to reemphasize the clarity criterion Held proposes. It is not the case that any conceivable collective action solution yields even a putative collective obligation. Only when the course of action presenting itself is clear to the reasonable person is it accurate to think in terms of the collective obligations of putative groups. Clarity at the collective level is a prerequisite for collective obligation in these cases, and that clarity serves as a lens through which the obligations of individuals come into focus.

Another possible objection is that these putative groups do not have any feature that allows us to recognize them as obligation-holding collectives. Decision procedures, organizational structures, and joint goals help to identify collective agents. The presence of a collective intention could contribute the requisite unifying feature, but in cases of inaction and putative groups, intentional collective action exists only as a potentiality. The collectives have not acknowledged themselves as collectives capable of acting together to achieve a jointly held goal or developed the structure required for forming collective intentions on which they might act. In response, I draw attention to two points. First, note that if the putative collective obligation becomes actual, the relevant obligation will be that of an organization or a goal-oriented collective. If the individuals who are potential members mobilize to act, the putative collective will transform into an actual one. And second, once again let us note the clarity condition. At the collective level, it must be clear what the potential collective agent will be and what it will do. Think of the Coordinated Bystander Case, where it is perfectly clear that the putative and (we hope) soon-to-be goal-oriented collective consists of the four individuals on the bank. The claim I have made throughout this chapter is that there is much more clarity between obligation and circumstance at the collective level than there is between individual obligation and circumstance when the only reasonable course of action is collective. In at least some cases, the identity of the putative collective will be clear. In others, it might not be as clear, and in still others, it won't be clear at all. Where the clarity condition is not met, there is no putative collective obligation through which to understand individual contributions.

Note, too, that in the middle ground between an obvious putative collective agent and none at all, we might invoke the idea of identifiable groups or collections of people whose connections to one another are loose—not nearly tight enough to ground any assumption of agency but not so unrelated that they share no significant features. Groups of this kind fall short with respect to agency because they lack an organizational structure or common goals that would provide a framework for intentional collective action. Nonetheless, they can be loosely identified in a way that is at least comparable to the way we identify random collections, for example the audience at the symphony. Affluent Westerners, for example, could fit this category. In chapter 1, I maintained that it's not helpful to hold groups such as affluent Westerners or privileged white men responsible for social problems such as poverty and oppression, on the grounds that these injustices and inequities are systemic and the explanations for their persistence require a more complex analysis than simply blaming one social group. Add to this their lack of an organizational structure or shared goal, and their lack of intentional agency seems apparent. At the same time, however, they are not simply mereological sums of completely unrelated people. In that respect, they are perhaps one step closer to potentially mobilizing as effective agents. And in fact, on occasion, they do. For example, affluent Westerners were in a position, through collective action, to assist the victims of the 2004 tsunami. Indeed, they rose to the occasion, banded together, and did make a difference. We witnessed the same thing after Hurricane Katrina in 2005. When individuals contributed, they did so as part of a collective venture; had they not, the average affluent Westerner would have felt the futility of her or his relatively small offering in the face of such vast destruction. Locating it as something done together with others, it takes on a heightened moral significance. Assume that if affluent North Americans mobilized as a group to donate a percentage of their wealth to humanitarian aid organizations, there would be a significant reduction in global poverty, disease, and hunger. Here we have an identifiable group—a putative collective agent—and a clear course of action. It may not be clear who all of the members of the group are, but at the collective level, both the group and the action are identifiable.

5.4 CONCLUSION

This chapter is meant to shed some light on the way that collective obligation can create possibilities for understanding obligation at the individual level when we are faced with challenges such as global warming, environmental degradation, widespread poverty, and malnutrition. These sorts of issues differ from situations created by organizations and goal-oriented collectives because they are not the products of collective agents. With respect to solutions, however, they mandate collective action. From an individual action perspective, these issues seem insurmountable. In the terms I have outlined, there is no direct mapping between individual obligation and the world circumstances in question. What do we do, then, when we recognize that when viewed from a collective perspective, these challenges demand collective solutions? When a clear collective solution emerges, I have argued that collective obligation can render individual obligations more determinate. In cases where the collective that might address the problem is putative rather than actual and the course of action this putative collective might take is clear, then the putative collective obligations associated with the solution have the same mediating role as actual collective obligations. Seen through the lens of collective obligation, even as a feature of a putative collective agent, individual actions and their impact as part of something larger become clearer. And while it is not the case that all seemingly insurmountable problems may be addressed in this manner, this account provides a starting point for how we might approach them.

[6]

INDIVIDUAL MORAL
RESPONSIBILITY IN WRONGFUL
SOCIAL PRACTICE

6.1 MORAL IGNORANCE AS AN EXCUSE

In the previous two chapters, my goal has been to understand the way collective contexts affect individual responsibility and obligation. In chapter 4, I claimed that while individuals are not responsible for collective acts as such, individuals can be responsible for their contributions to collective acts. Moreover, I maintained, in order to appreciate adequately the moral dimensions of individual acts in collective action contexts, it is necessary to recognize them as contributions to collective acts. Chapter 5 explored the relationship between collective and individual obligation, especially in cases that do not arise from collective action but call for collective action solutions. I argued that collective obligation gives form and order to individual obligation even when the collective agents and obligations are putative instead of actual. I proposed that a slightly modified version of Held's position that putative agents or random collections can have obligations to act when the course of collective action is clear to the reasonable person would be adequate to the task.

I maintained that the obligations accruing to putative collective agents are themselves putative. Regardless, clear courses of collective action can present themselves, and these have a potentially binding effect on individuals who would be members of putative collective agents.

Not all situations satisfy the condition of clarity to the reasonable person where collective action solutions are concerned. In those cases lacking clarity, individuals are not going to be able to locate their moral possibilities within a collective action solution because there are none apparent. One such circumstance in which there is a notable lack of clarity occurs when wrongful social practice is the status quo and there is widespread ignorance at both the collective and individual levels of the wrongness or the harmfulness. Racist, sexist, homophobic, and other discriminatory practices that perpetuate oppression or lead to the exploitation of groups of people fall into this category. When ways of life are uncritically accepted as legitimate, individuals routinely participate in practices of whose wrongness they are ignorant. If conditions of clarity can obligate, then perhaps conditions in which clarity is lacking and ignorance abounds might excuse. My goal in this chapter is to consider the extent to which ignorance at the collective level may be a legitimate excuse for individuals who contribute to wrongful social practices. At the same time, we do not want to lose sight of the value of collective action solutions even when they are not immediately apparent. Sometimes, solutions that are not clear eventually become so. We want an analysis of responsibility in conditions of collective moral ignorance to leave room for a transition from a state of moral ignorance to a state of moral knowledge.

My discussion focuses on wrongful, not just harmful, social practice. Though there is reason to invoke collective action solutions in response to either case, and lack of clarity might equally cloud our ability to see our way to a solution in either case, the greater moral risk to individuals resides in situations in which their contributions are actually wrong. Wrongs that occur as part of social practice may occur in circumstances in which "social acceptance of a practice impedes the individual's awareness of wrongdoing."[1] Social conditions of acceptance can put agents at moral risk, in the sense that they are at risk of doing what is wrong where they do not intend any wrongdoing. In such situations, they are susceptible to ascriptions of blame. Oppressive social practice—discrimination, exploitation, and subordination of people on the basis of their membership in a particular social group—is wrong and unjust.

The issues raised here are both similar to and different from the issues addressed in chapter 4 in attempting to determine how to assign individual responsibility in cases of intentional collective wrongdoing involving organizations and goal-oriented collectives. They are similar because the collective element both of group action contexts and of social practice contexts complicates responsibility at the individual level. They are different because cultures do not, strictly speaking, act, so there is no wrongful collective action to isolate. Instead, the wrong in the cultural examples involve unjust patterns of social practice. This characterization of them makes it difficult to establish agency, or even potential agency, at the collective level. Furthermore, individuals typically do not recognize their contributions as part of a pattern of injustice, and so are not intentionally contributing to it. These are important differences that take the discussion in a different direction, namely, to the impact on individual responsibility of widespread ignorance of wrongful social practice.

My discussion rests on the assumption that we are all to some extent influenced by the cultural context in which we live. Our social and cultural environment determines, in large part, the values, attitudes, and fundamental beliefs we have available to us and embrace. Of course the social/cultural context does not fully determine how we think and act, but the context of a social practice is a collective setting that may operate as a mitigating circumstance with respect to individual moral responsibility, thus alleviating individual blame. Assuming that widespread acceptance of a practice is not sufficient to make the practice morally permissible, but granting that cultures influence the values and behaviors of individuals, I want to consider what impact, if any, this fact of cultural influence has on the moral responsibility of individuals with respect to blameworthiness for their part in wrongs that fit into a scheme of culturally accepted practices that is not recognized as wrong. I argue that conditions of widespread ignorance can, in fact, constitute an adequate excuse at the individual level, thus alleviating blame. Having an excuse does not mean that the behavior is morally acceptable. Unlike justification, in which an action that might ordinarily be considered wrong turns out to be permissible, excuse leaves moral wrongness intact but mitigates blame.

Despite ignorance at the collective level serving, under appropriate conditions, as an excuse for responsibility at the individual level, we want to leave room for some mechanism for change. In the previous chapter, we saw that collective solutions can materialize when we have our sights on putative groups. In the situations here under discussion, clarity even of the problem is, by hypothesis, absent to the majority of people involved. Getting a solution off the ground will, therefore, require a shift from moral ignorance to moral knowledge.

Before I begin my discussion of ignorance as a possible excuse, I want to draw attention to—only for the purpose of setting it aside—the proposal that this social and cultural influence of which I speak can generate a cognitive inability to understand and appreciate the world for what it is, particularly with respect to some range of moral phenomena. Some might wish to argue that, given that "ought implies can," we might explain diminished responsibility in cases of individual participation in socially accepted practices that are wrong as based in inability.[2] According to this view, when individuals internalize the set of values embodied by their culture, they may end up lacking the ability to perceive some moral phenomena in ways that adequately reflect the moral facts. If agents lack the ability to tell right from wrong within a certain range of cases, then we have an explanation for why they are not morally responsible for acts within that range. This analysis captures the intuition that the influence of a culture on individuals raised in its context can impede the ability to see what is right and what is wrong, and justifies the claim of diminished responsibility. I much favor an analysis based on widespread moral ignorance within a culture, rather than on a culturally generated inability. Ignorance more accurately reflects the complexity of the phenomena while still supporting our intuitions concerning influence and responsibility. Moreover, an inability might be dangerously impervious to remedy, whereas the project of replacing moral ignorance with moral knowledge, though not easy, is at least approachable.

In order to provide an analysis that supports mechanisms for social progress, we need to specify some conditions under which it is appropriate not to excuse individuals for certain behaviors and attitudes even if the individuals are products of a culture in which harmful patterns are entrenched. There must be some conditions under which, despite widespread social acceptance of some practice that is wrong, it is possible for individuals engaging in that practice to be morally responsible for their participation. In order for this to be possible, it cannot be the case that the influence of culture is totalizing and absolute.

In what follows, I will address first the idea of affected ignorance, which I argue is not a sound basis for excuse. Next, I invoke a useful distinction, first introduced by Cheshire Calhoun, between normal and abnormal moral contexts and explain that ignorance about moral wrongness in a normal moral context does not excuse, whereas ignorance in abnormal moral contexts does. Finally, I consider mechanisms for shifting the context from ignorance to clarity, thereby opening the door to collective action solutions.

6.2 AFFECTED IGNORANCE

Not all sources of ignorance will constitute a good excuse. Most of us believe the commonsense idea that sometimes a person who does something wrong "should have known better." We regularly shame children with that common admonishment, and think it quietly to ourselves with respect to adult behavior from time to time as well. One category of ignorance we are especially loath to excuse— and rightly so—is that of affected or motivated ignorance. Michelle Moody-Adams argues that we should reject the idea that cultural ignorance could ever constitute a sound moral excuse for individuals.[3] Invoking the example of slavery in ancient Greece, she notes that while some people have claimed that it would have been very difficult for the people in that society to question the practice because within the culture there was no substantial moral criticism of the practice, it is hardly surprising that the literature objecting to an accepted social practice would have difficulty surviving.[4] Moody-Adams suggests that "the belief that slavery was justified was insufficiently examined by those who held it" and claims that their ignorance of wrongdoing was simply affected ignorance. Affected ignorance is "choosing not to know whether some practice in which one participates might be wrong."⁵ We might equally well think of this as willful or motivated ignorance, since in the typical case there is a self-interested reason for evading moral knowledge that might require one to rethink one's way of life. For example, in ancient Greece slave owners clearly had an interest in maintaining the institution of slavery from which they reaped so many benefits. The charge of affected ignorance introduces an element of choice concerning the ignorance, and thus captures an idea that the individuals who participate in these wrongful practices remain intentionally ignorant of the practices' wrongness, and so are in some sense responsible for their actions with respect to these practices, even though they are doing what is culturally acceptable. Note that affected ignorance, at least in the situations under discussion here, is a feature of individuals, not collective agents. Although it could be a feature of organizations and goal-oriented collectives—they have intentional mechanisms that facilitate choice—the requisite intentional capacity required is not attributable to cultures or societies because they lack the structural features of agents.

When ignorance of one's participation in wrongful behavior is indeed affected, then it can hardly constitute a sound moral excuse. Moody-Adams believes, however, that widespread cultural practice, as difficult as it might make it to understand the nature of one's wrongdoing, never provides an adequate ground for ignorance as an excuse. She thinks that allowing it as an excuse does not give enough intellectual credit to members of societies that engage in morally corrupt social practices. She argues that we do best when we take the stance of "the forgiving moralist," in which we acknowledge how difficult it is to go against the social grain but countenance that it is not impossible. Moody-Adams cites evidence from a 1956 experiment in which Solomon Asch studied people's conformity in perceptual judgments. Owen Flanagan describes the experiment:

"Subjects were asked to determine which of two lines in a series of pairs was longer. The correct choices were sufficiently unambiguous so that members of control groups performed perfectly. But in groups where the subject was the sixth or seventh in line after persons intentionally making the wrong choice, one-third conformed to absurd, perceptually unconscionable judgments."[6] That one-third of the subjects in the experiment conformed to these absurd judgments indicates that many people are willing to conform to majority opinion even when this opinion is obviously wrong. However, two-thirds did not so conform. This fact provides encouraging support for the view that nonconformity may be uncomfortable and difficult, but it is psychologically possible for most people. The attitude of the forgiving moralist allows us to forgive but not excuse conformist behavior that we should know is wrong. Holding individuals to a higher moral standard than the status quo that they and their fellows practice allows us to expect more from others and ourselves, thus opening the door for moral progress.

We can conclude from this discussion that the charge of affected ignorance might apply in some cases. Where it does, ignorance is no excuse. Nonetheless, it is unreasonable to think that every case of widespread moral ignorance about the wrongness of some cultural practice must be a case of affected ignorance. Some cases of ignorance may be genuinely nonculpable rather than affected (though admittedly forgivable). Recall that sometimes moral ignorance can put people at moral risk who in all sincerity aim to act rightly. It is simply not reasonable to think that everyone at all times and in all locations has equal access to the full range of actual and possible moral knowledge. Some advances in moral knowledge may be analogous in relevant ways to advances in other kinds of knowledge such as knowledge of the natural world. Some of the things we know, for example, that the planet Earth is round, are things that we could only come to know given a certain stage in the history of knowledge. Perhaps some moral knowledge is like that, and so ignorance of some of the facts is genuine. Furthermore, as with other kinds of knowledge, once moral discoveries are made, they are not immediately known or knowable by everyone. It takes some time for knowledge to become commonplace. Some advances in knowledge, moral or otherwise, are significant human achievements that do not come to us easily.[7] The claim that moral ignorance of the wrongness of some cultural practice must always be affected (even if understandable) does not acknowledge that moral knowledge, like other forms of knowledge, unfolds in a process of discovery. In the next section, I consider how we might make room for evolution in moral thinking, thus providing a basis for the claim that sometimes widespread ignorance constitutes a genuine excuse.

6.3 NORMAL AND ABNORMAL MORAL CONTEXTS

Cheshire Calhoun introduces the distinction between moral knowledge in a normal moral context and moral knowledge in an abnormal moral context. This distinction is useful for understanding when moral ignorance that stems from widespread ignorance concerning the moral status of accepted practice could constitute an acceptable excuse for individuals. In a normal moral context, "rightness and wrongness of different courses of action is 'transparent' to individuals, where 'transparent' does not mean self-evident, but simply that participants in normal moral contexts share a common moral language, agree for the most part on moral rules, and use similar methods of moral reasoning."[8] In normal contexts, we expect people to be familiar with the language, the rules, and the principles of their moral community, as well as expecting them to be familiar with what the rules apply to (e.g., promises, respect, pollution, etc.). Ignorance in these contexts is ignorance of what the moral community in general knows. In this respect, ignorance in a normal moral context differs from ignorance in an abnormal one.

"Abnormal moral contexts," states Calhoun, "arise at the frontiers of moral knowledge when a subgroup of society (e.g., bioethicists or business ethicists) makes advances in moral knowledge faster than they can be disseminated to and assimilated by the general public and the subgroup at moral risk (e.g., physicians, corporate executives). As a result the rightness or wrongness of some courses of action (for example, routine involuntary sterilization of the mentally ill) are, for a time, transparent only to the knowledge-acquiring subgroup but 'opaque' to outsiders."[9] As an example, Calhoun cites most feminist moral critique, which she claims occurs in abnormal moral contexts (e.g., the claim that "he" is not gender neutral, and that its continued use as a gender-neutral term excludes women, thereby contributing to their oppression). Only a limited range of people grasp the moral import of the social criticism feminists make. Ignorance in the abnormal moral context occurs at the social level, making it extremely challenging to identify and address.

Calhoun suggests that when ignorance occurs in an abnormal moral context, we should have "diminished expectations" because there is just no reason, outside the knowledge-acquiring subgroup, for people to know. There is no recognition of a moral dimension to the behavior or practice in question. When moral ignorance of a particular range of moral judgments takes place in an abnormal moral context, individuals have an excuse sufficient to mitigate their blameworthiness. Although the agents have fully developed critical skills and are generally responsible agents, their ignorance is of new moral categories that have not been absorbed by the general population. Thus, they are not responsible for it or for wrongs that flow from it.

Given her analysis, Calhoun maintains that it may not be appropriate to blame, to hold responsible, for example, "the ordinary man" for using "he" gender neutrally or calling women "girls." These practices take on a moral dimension when they are viewed through the eyes of feminist social critics, and that creates an abnormal context with respect to these practices because the critical framework is not recognized by the dominant culture. These "ordinary men" aren't party to information that they would need in order to recognize this behavior as contributing to oppression (nor, indeed, are many "ordinary women"). To the extent that this is true, it would be inappropriate to hold them responsible as individuals. It is arguable that in cases that resemble this one in the relevant respects, the new moral ideas will be thoroughly different in emphasis from the old ones and will require significant revisions in the way things are conceptualized. Where recognition of morally wrong practice requires a shift in perspective, the acquisition of new information does not come easily.[10]

In the previous chapter, I argued that we should adopt the normative standard of the reasonable person proposed by Held as a criterion for determining when collective action solutions might take on the character of obligations or putative obligations with a derivative binding and sorting effect on the obligations of individuals. In the context of Calhoun's distinction, we can think of clarity to the reasonable person as obtaining in a normal moral context. In a context that is normal with respect to global warming, for example, it is widely recognized as a collective problem to which we need to turn our attention. Conversely, when ignorance occurs in an abnormal moral context, we may invoke the clarity condition to explain why it should excuse individuals from blame. In an abnormal moral context, the reasonable person cannot be expected to have a full grasp of the moral contours of her behavior, of the problem in which it is embedded, or of the collective action solution (should one exist) that would address it. If Calhoun is correct, then we exist in an abnormal moral context with respect to feminist critique. Moral critiques of social contexts of oppression and exploitation more generally occur in abnormal moral contexts. Only a small group of people recognize and countenance the content and legitimacy of these critiques.

If moral ignorance in an abnormal moral context meets the reasonable person criterion, it excuses. We can assume that cases of affected ignorance will fail the reasonable person test: a reasonable person will not affect ignorance in the name of personal benefit. Having determined that ignorance in these cases can excuse, we need now to consider what mechanisms for altering the range of knowledge exist. In order to make the transition from abnormal to normal moral contexts, there must be ways of educating people who are in a state of ignorance about their participation in wrongful social practices. In the next section, I consider ways in which blameworthy individuals may nonetheless be held to account for their behavior.

6.4 BLAME, REPROACH, AND DIALOGUE

If the abnormal moral context excuses individuals and if the collective context in which the ignorance abounds lacks the structural features that make it a moral agent, then we may seem stuck in current social circumstances, because no one will be responsible. But moral progress occurs when there is a shift from an abnormal to a normal moral context with respect to a given issue. Once that shift occurs, appeals to ignorance no longer serve as adequate bases for an excuse. What measures may be taken to address morally wrong behavior for which individuals are excused? It bears emphasis that excuse is not the same as justification. Recall the distinction. Excused behavior remains wrong, whereas justified behavior is permitted. For example, self-defense is considered by many to be justified killing, not at all wrong. If someone has an excuse for killing, the act itself remains wrong, but the agent is not to be blamed. That the behavior remains wrong opens the door for action to be taken, if not against the individual then at a minimum as a corrective. In what follows, I consider the roles of reproach and of dialogue in bringing about shifts from abnormal to normal moral contexts.

Assume, as Calhoun has assumed, that at least some individuals in an abnormal moral context have access to advances in moral knowledge. Then there is room for pointing out the moral mistakes of others. Individuals may not be responsible, but they may still be reproached, claims Calhoun. In fact, she believes it essential that the wrongness be pointed out to the offender. Silence has the effect of sanctioning the behavior, because it does not give the offender any reason to think he has misstepped.[11] Calhoun suggests reproach as a good mechanism for accomplishing this change. It means pointing out that what they have done is wrong and letting them know their part in a larger scheme of wrongful practice. Calhoun suggests that the most effective form this reproach may take is as a kind of labeling. If someone, even if unknowingly, exploits, then that person is an "exploiter." Those who violate rights are "rights violators"; those who oppress are "oppressors."[12] Using language that identifies them as such, rather than language that excuses the behavior, draws "attention both to self-legislative capacities and to the moral obligatoriness of not participating in oppressive social behavior," and is appropriate even when social conditions are sufficient to mitigate responsibility.[13] Thus, where the behavior takes place in an abnormal moral context, "our entitlement to use reproach is independent of the blameworthiness of individuals."[14] Recall that the goal is to create a shift in moral context from abnormal, in which ignorance constitutes an excuse, to normal, in which ignorance no longer constitutes an excuse. The effect of consistent reproach is to alter the balance of knowledge and ignorance. If individuals who transgress are regularly reproached for their transgressions, even if gently and with an eye to their blamelessness, they will no longer be ignorant, even if the context remains abnormal for some time. But moreover, as more people gain the knowledge, the change will eventually come. If using sexist language regularly saddles people with the label "sexist," they might eventually come to understand the point and might even eventually come around. At a minimum, they will lose their excuse.

Engaging people in dialogue in order to explain the moral concern is another approach that could generate the requisite shift. The suggestion of a dialogue will seem overly optimistic if we expect immediate change. It would be unreasonable to expect an abnormal context to become normal overnight. The change is gradual. And this is where affected ignorance plays a part. Perhaps even more so than with respect to reproach, which has a better chance than dialogue of generating backlash and resistance, the more insistent people are in initiating and advancing dialogue, the less it will be possible for individuals to be given refuge from responsibility in the abnormal context. Even within the abnormal moral context, individual cases—and gradually more and more of them—will arise in which appeal to the context will no longer ground diminished expectation, and so will not ground diminished responsibility. At some point, the lingering ignorance of some members of the group at moral risk is more likely to be affected than it is genuine. Consider again writers with respect to the issue of nonsexist language. Few people who write for a living can actually claim to be ignorant of the issue of nonsexist language; by now they likely have a view about the matter, and whatever their view, they must recognize it as a morally charged issue. It is no longer possible seriously to claim, "Well, I was always taught that 'he' is gender neutral, and no one has ever suggested otherwise." Thus, writers are in less of a position to appeal to ignorance in an abnormal moral context than others with respect to this issue.

So far, the picture looks like this: a shift from an abnormal moral context to a normal moral context with respect to some issues takes place when members of knowledge-acquiring subgroups—the experts "on the frontiers of moral knowledge"—bring new knowledge discoveries to nonmembers. As the context shifts, ignorance of wrongdoing loses its status as an excuse for individuals participating in social practices that are wrong. Two refinements to this understanding are in order. First, let us dispel the image of teams of experts working in laboratory settings to make advances in moral knowledge. Of course there are moral experts—bioethicists, legal ethicists, feminist ethicists, business ethicists—and their work advances our moral thinking. At the same time, however, it makes sense to suppose that at least some members of the general population, particularly but not exclusively some members of disadvantaged groups who are suffering the burdens of wrongful social practice, have insights into the injustices even if they are not moral "experts" in the business of developing new moral categories and even if they are relatively powerless to do anything about it.[15] Women, slaves, members of targeted racial and ethnic groups, disabled individuals— they do not need moral experts to understand that there is something troubling and unjust about their situation. Artists of all kinds, from filmmakers to poets, are another sector whose insights and observations introduce new frameworks for thinking about morality. A more inclusive account of where new moral knowledge might originate better captures the diversity of the forces of change. It also provides more promise, in that it sees the seeds of change scattered more widely, not limited to the results of research pursued in ivory towers.

Second, the account implies a uniformity of belief among members of the subgroup—with respect to the relevant issues—that we should not in reality expect.[16] Bioethicists disagree among themselves; business ethicists disagree among themselves; feminists disagree among themselves. Given the undeniable fact of disagreement, we need to make sense of the claim that judgments that are opaque to the rest of the population are transparent to members of the knowledge-acquiring subgroup. If there is disagreement about certain issues, we cannot very well claim that members of the subgroup, as a group, possess knowledge. In response, note that moral disagreement in abnormal contexts would only pose a difficulty if the transparency that we expect is transparency of particular judgments. Transparency of particular judgments does not capture what is important in the distinction between normal and abnormal moral contexts. We may say that what makes a context abnormal is that an issue that some minority of people recognize as morally charged is not recognized as a moral issue at all by the general population. The basis for the claim that an appeal to ignorance grounds diminished responsibility with respect to participation in wrongful social practices is not typically the assumption that agents did what was wrong thinking it right; the claim of diminished responsibility rests on the assumption that the agent did not realize that there was any moral issue at all. For example, while feminists may disagree about whether wearing makeup supports an industry that perpetuates the oppression of women, they share as a subgroup the recognition that it is an issue with moral dimensions. This recognition sets them apart and makes some of the issues that they discuss atypical with respect to the general population. The prevailing absence of recognition that these issues have an importantly moral component makes the social context in which people are ignorant of them abnormal. Something's becoming transparent as an issue need not amount to transparency about what to say about the issue, though for some issues (e.g., slavery) particular judgments will become transparent eventually as well. Viewed in this way, disagreement among members of knowledge-acquiring subgroups does not undermine the idea of an abnormal moral context. Indeed, it makes good sense to think that the introduction of new issues would generate some disagreement among those who take them up for discussion.

Does the prospect of disagreement about issues pose a challenge for the conditions under which a shift from abnormal to normal moral context might take place? I raise this question because, at the outset, we were concerned with conditions for responsibility for participation in cultural practices that are wrong. The abnormal moral context is meant to explain the circumstances under which individuals who participate in these practices are not morally responsible for this wrong behavior. But on closer scrutiny, we have seen that it is not a straightforward matter of some people possessing knowledge of wrongness that most people lack. For "at the frontiers of moral knowledge" there will not always be agreement. Thus, we need to ask what the members of the subgroups bring to the general population in order to normalize the abnormal context, in order to make people more accountable for their participation in practices that are or may be wrong. Consider, for a moment, Calhoun's suggestion that reproach is an appropriate approach to facilitating a shift in context. This process is to assist people in coming to see things in the way that the members of the knowledge-acquiring subgroup do. Attending to the existence of disagreement, however, raises questions concerning the conditions under which reproach is appropriate. For if the matter is not settled even among those who are aware of the issue, there will be different judgments—originating from within the knowledge-acquiring subgroups—about the rightness or wrongness of certain practices. The suggestion of dialogue as an alternative to reproach helps to address this concern. Where there is not uniform agreement, those who have some insight into the issue should try to convey to others an awareness of the issue and information about the relevant moral questions and the relevant points of view. The idea is to bring more people into the dialogue, to urge more people to examine what was previously unexamined. Keep in mind that the ultimate aim is to normalize an abnormal moral context so that people will have to be more accountable for their behavior where their participation in a morally questionable though culturally accepted practice is concerned. In a normal moral context, most people realize or see the morally relevant features of situations; the relevant features are not opaque. For example, we recognize that spousal abuse is wrong, that slavery is morally impermissible, that, other things being equal, promises ought to be kept. In these cases, the judgments are transparent to the general population. But we also realize that abortion and euthanasia, the ethics of eating meat, and the moral status of sex work are morally charged issues with various morally relevant features that different people weigh differently. If we understand that part of the process of progressive social change is disseminating knowledge to the general population so that an abnormal context becomes a normal one, it does not much matter whether the knowledge is reasonably definitive or whether a new dialogue is introduced. The main point is to force attentiveness in agents who are already, for the most part, morally reflective or sensitive. A shift in context renders judgments or issues transparent that were once opaque to a large portion of the population. We achieve this shift when individuals come to see themselves as responsible.

The two refinements discussed here—the broadening of prospects for where new moral knowledge might be produced or discovered and the recognition that attentiveness to issues, about which there might be some moral disagreement, is a step forward in changing a context from abnormal to normal—help to explain how the process of change happens. Thus, despite ignorance in abnormal moral contexts constituting an excuse, there are sufficient means of facilitating a transition out of an abnormal moral context that excusing individuals from blame does not mean that nothing can be done.

Of course, at times, ignorance will be affected. When ignorance is affected, rather than being a function of an abnormal moral context, individuals will be blameworthy unless other mitigating factors are present. Other mitigating conditions may also have to do with the cultural context, but they are not to be identified with nonculpable ignorance. For example, the accepted culture may create difficulties in doing what one ought that do not amount to difficulties in knowing what one ought to do. Coercive conditions that generate fear of the consequences of noncompliance, for example, those that might have existed in Nazi Germany, may be relevant considerations.[17] The difficulty created by coercive conditions is a good explanation for why it may seem prudent to affect ignorance of what is being done, and so may be a good explanation for why some cases of affected ignorance seem less blameworthy than others.

6.5 CONCLUSION

We may regard the issue concerning the connection between context, ignorance, and responsibility as variable with respect to scope, particularly the scope of the context. When we put the question in terms of the impact that culturally dependent ignorance has on responsibility, we are isolating a relatively wide, collective context. In any particular situation, our own epistemic limitations put us in a position in which we can never be certain that we have all that we need to make the correct judgment. Various sorts of things may interfere with our judgment even if we are reasonably reflective, and cultural presuppositions may be one of them. Thus, we are at any time at moral risk.[18] In recognition of our limited ability to access all of the relevant facts, or to know how these facts ought to be weighed in a given situation, some moral theorists distinguish between what is actually right to do and what an agent is right to do given what she knows about the situation and given that she has been reasonably reflective.[19] In situations where agents act wrongly on the basis of ignorance that is understandable given the context, it is plausible to believe that, even in acting wrongly, they are not morally responsible.

My purpose throughout this chapter has been to address widespread ignorance and individual blameworthiness in a way that supports the possibility of social change and that suggests mechanisms by which this may be accomplished through the dissemination of moral knowledge. I have suggested that insistent dialogue is a more promising means of achieving changes than reproach, though at times reproach will effectively make the point. I do not claim to have exhausted the ways in which to achieve advances.

When a change takes hold, new moral understandings become clear. Sometimes new moral understandings can bring to light possibilities for collective action that were previously unrecognized.

Sometimes, blurry and then increasingly clearer edges will begin to form around putative groups, and the obligations at that level may, as explained in the previous chapter, help to narrow down the moral possibilities that individuals see for themselves. Then, individuals who are able to understand their moral position in the context of a larger effort have the means available to them to understand themselves as and to become, together with others, effective agents of change.

CONCLUSION

We incline toward blame when we think of collective moral responsibility, turning our minds most often to wrongdoing and negligence: the Holocaust; genocide in Rwanda and Darfur; corporate wrongdoing and corruption at Enron;[1] organizational negligence at Union Carbide in Bhopal, India,[2] at the Canadian Red Cross, within the Catholic Church.[3] Today's news in the summer of 2010 asks about the extent of BP's blameworthiness and liability for the disastrous oil leak in the Gulf of Mexico.[4] Throughout 2010, Toyota has scrambled to protect its reputation (and its customers) in the wake of massive recalls due to safety concerns.[5] Collective moral responsibility is not, however, only about blame. We can tell some good news stories of praiseworthy collective action, too: successful mobilization of humanitarian relief after the 2006 tsunami in Southeast Asia, Hurricane Katrina on the Gulf Coast of the United States in 2007, and the 2009 earthquake in Haiti; increased awareness leading to "greener" communities and an emphasis on the reduction of landfill and an increase in recycling; the women's movement; the dismantling in South Africa of apartheid, the system of institutionalized racism in effect between 1948 and 1994, and the election of Nelson Mandela as president of South Africa in 1994; the election of Barack Obama as president of the United States in 2008. These successes remind us that in the face of seemingly insurmountable problems, the possibility of collective solutions gives us reason to hope.

My main goal in this book has been philosophical: to develop and defend a two-level view of moral responsibility, with an eye to accounting for moral responsibility in collective contexts. According to this view, moral responsibility occurs at the collective level and the individual level. In other words, both collective agents and individual human agents qualify as responsible moral agents to whom ascriptions of praise and blame apply. In the introduction, I outlined a number of cases—genocide in Rwanda, the Canadian Red Cross and the tainted blood scandal, global warming, wrongful social practice and oppression—to which I have referred from time to time to help illustrate and motivate my view. The view I outline does not, however, depend on any one particular case or even type of case. I offer it as a philosophical framework for thinking through cases of collective moral responsibility, of individual moral responsibility in collective contexts, and of collective obligation and its relation to individual obligation. I maintain throughout that action and moral responsibility operate at two different levels, that of the individual and that of the collective, and that though these levels might inform each other in some ways, they are importantly distinct. In chapter 1, I outlined a view of intentional collective action according to which two kinds of collective agents, organizations and goal-oriented collectives, have intentional structures that support agency. In my view, the existence of these structures independently provides sufficient ground for collective moral responsibility.

Nevertheless, recognizing that many people object to the idea of collective agency, I argued in chapter 2 that in addition to having independent metaphysical reasons for treating collective agents as moral agents, there are further normative reasons for doing so. When collectives' actions, either conceptually or de facto, are not the acts of any one individual, and when the acts in their entirety have a moral dimension that is not captured in the contribution of any individual contribution, there is a normative loss if we do not countenance collective moral responsibility for the whole. Moreover, I argued, the loss transmits further to the individual level of moral evaluation because individual contributions take on different moral dimensions when they are understood as contributions to the larger whole. Fundraisers and genocides, I claimed, can have this character under appropriate conditions.

Many misconceptions concerning collective moral responsibility and collective guilt lead people to reject them out of hand. In both chapters 2 and 3, I have attempted to clear up some of these confusions, firmly believing that once cleared up, collective moral responsibility and collective guilt will appear more plausible to those who might previously have rejected them. The main point I stress throughout is that there is no necessary connection between collective moral responsibility and the responsibility of individuals who are members of blameworthy or praiseworthy collectives. People worry more about the prospect of individuals being blamed for the actions of others, so I spend more time making it clear that this is not a necessary feature of collective responsibility on the two-level model. On the contrary, the two-level theory draws a sharp distinction between intention, action, and moral responsibility at the collective level and intention, action, and moral responsibility at the individual level.

The sharp distinction does not, however, mean that individuals who take part in blameworthy collective endeavors are automatically absolved of responsibility when collective blame is established. Though the levels are distinct, there is interplay between them, and though individuals are not responsible for the collective actions in which they play a part, they most certainly can be responsible in the collective actions to which they contribute. They are responsible for their contributions. Chapter 4 unpacked the complexity of individual responsibility in collective action scenarios, focusing on individual responsibility in organizations and goal-oriented collective agents. Again I discussed the importance of conceiving of individual contributions as contributions to collective efforts, this time in the context of Davidsonian action theory and the idea of the "accordion effect." Some of our individual actions can be described in more expansive terms, and these terms can include their contributions to collective actions. Some of these collective action descriptions draw our attention to morally relevant qualities of the action, thus highlighting moral features of individual contributions that would otherwise be invisible.

Collective obligation lends shape and form to individual obligation under certain conditions, or so I argued in chapter 5. Some of the more challenging issues facing us today are not the products of collective agency yet clearly require collective action solutions. I look at a continuum of cases in which the solution and the agent who might undertake the solution get increasingly less clear. I claim that in some cases, the clear solution involves a putative rather than actual collective agent. In these clear cases, the putative collective obligations can have the same impact on individual obligations as actual collective obligations, that is, putative obligations can render more determinate the range of individual alternatives available to those who would participate in potential collective action solutions.

The course of action will not always be clear. Sometimes, whole communities, cultures, or societies engage in social practices that are wrong and not widely known to be wrong. Individuals who take part, even well-meaning individuals who have an interest in doing the right thing, are at risk of doing the wrong thing out of ignorance. The guiding question in chapter 6 is whether this kind of ignorance can ever serve as a legitimate excuse for wrongful behavior. I claim that under appropriate conditions, namely when the ignorance occurs in an abnormal moral context, it can excuse. I also consider mechanisms for creating a shift from an abnormal moral context to a normal one. Individuals may not always be blameworthy for their ignorance, but they may certainly be called to account. As the context undergoes a transition, ignorance no longer excuses, and there is hope for social change.

Given my conclusions, a number of issues arise that I have given little attention here and will turn to in future work. Primary among them is an investigation of how to proceed after finding a collective agent blameworthy. Collective punishment and alternatives to it, such as reparations, compensation schemes, truth commissions, are rich areas of discussion for philosophers, political scientists, and legal scholars.[6]

The potential for moral progress is the one strength of my view with which I would like to conclude. As I stated at the outset, my view does not simply provide a conceptual framework, though that is one of its main features. It also offers a way that human beings, as moral agents, may think about themselves in relation to others. I argue that seeing ourselves in this way increases our range of moral opportunities and also our range of moral obligations. One of the main moral demons of our time is the moral indifference that stems, in part, from the sense that, as an individual, I cannot and do not make a difference. One of the hopes that I have for this book is that readers will be encouraged by my account to see themselves more clearly in relation to the collectives of which they are parts. In articulating the importance of collective moral responsibility and showing how collective contexts shape individual moral responsibility, I provide an uncomplicated framework within which we may better understand our agency within the complex of collective contexts in which we function. Seeing how the collective and the individual levels of responsibility function alongside each other can dispel moral indifference in at least two ways. First, it can make us, as individuals, more aware that some of our actions are, in fact, contributions to blameworthy collective wrongdoing, making these actions and us, as their agents, candidates for blameworthiness. And second, it can awaken us to the morally empowering view that, together with others, we can make a moral difference after all.

NOTES

Introduction

1. Roméo Dallaire, *Shake Hands with the Devil* (Toronto: Random House, 2003), p. 47.
2. See ibid.; Philip Gourevitch, *We Wish to Inform You That Tomorrow We Will Be Killed with Our Families: Stories from Rwanda* (New York: Farrar, Straus and Giroux, 1998); Nigel Eltringham, *Accounting for Horror: Post-genocide Debates in Rwanda* (London: Pluto Press, 2004).
3. Eltringham, *Accounting for Horror*, p. 1.
4. André Picard, *The Gift of Death: Confronting Canada's Tainted-Blood Tragedy* (Toronto: HarperCollins, 1995).
5. Ibid., p. 1.
6. Ibid.
7. Tracy Isaacs, "Feminism and Agency," in *Feminist Moral Philosophy*, ed. Samantha Brennan, *Canadian Journal of Philosophy* supp. vol. 28 (Calgary: University of Calgary Press, 2003), pp. 129–54.
8. Chapter 5.
9. Chapter 5.
10. Genocide is an interesting example because in international law the Convention on the Prevention and Punishment of the Crime of Genocide clearly establishes criteria according to which an individual may commit an "act of genocide." Nonetheless, I argue that the normative significance of genocide derives from its scope as a collective atrocity befalling a group and being perpetrated by a group.

11. Leslie Green, "Legal Obligation and Authority," in *Stanford Encyclopedia of Philosophy*, spring 2004 ed., ed. Edward N. Zalta, http://plato.stanford.edu/archives/spr2004/entries/legal-obligation/.

12. Some frequently cited authors on these topics are John Martin Fischer, Harry G. Frankfurt, Peter Strawson, Peter Van Inwagen, and Gary Watson. An excellent source for canonical essays in the field is Gary Watson, ed., *Free Will*, 2nd ed. (Oxford: Oxford University Press, 2003).

13. Gary Watson, introduction to ibid., pp. 1–25, p. 2.

14. Some examples include David Copp, "What Collectives Are: Agency, Individualism, and Legal Theory," *Dialogue* 23 (1984): 249–69; Peter French, "The Corporation as a Moral Person," *American Philosophical Quarterly* 16, 3 (1979): 207–15; Larry May, *The Morality of Groups* (Notre Dame, Ind.: University of Notre Dame Press, 1987); and essays anthologized in *Collective Responsibility*, ed. Larry May and Stacey Hoffman (Savage, Md.: Rowman and Littlefield, 1991).

15. See, for example, H. D. Lewis, "Collective Responsibility," in May and Hoffman, *Collective Responsibility*, pp. 17–33, and Jan Narveson, "Collective Responsibility," *Journal of Ethics* 6, 2 (2002): 179–98.

16. See Peter French, "The Corporation as a Moral Person," *American Philosophical Quarterly* 16 (1979): 207–15; D. E. Cooper, "Collective Responsibility," in May and Hoffman, *Collective Responsibility*, pp. 35–46; David Copp, "On the Agency of Certain Collective Entities: An Argument from 'Normative Autonomy,'" *Midwest Studies in Philosophy* 30, 1 (2006): 194–221.

17. French, "The Corporation as a Moral Person."

18. See Gregory Mellema, *Collective Responsibility* (Amsterdam: Rodopi Press, 1997).

19. See Lewis, "Collective Responsibility," and Narveson, "Collective Responsibility."

20. See my arguments in chapters 2 and 4.

Chapter 1: Intentional Collective Action

1. Peggy McIntosh, "White Privilege: Unpacking the Invisible Backpack," in *White Privilege and Male Privilege: A Personal Account of Coming to See Correspondences through Work in Women's Studies*, working paper 189 (Wellesley, Mass.: Wellesley College Center for Research on Women, 1988); Chandra Mohanty, *Feminism without Borders* (Durham, N.C.: Duke University Press, 2003); Uma Narayan, *Dislocating Cultures: Identities, Traditions, and Third World Feminism* (New York: Routledge, 1997); Sandra Bartky, "In Defense of Guilt," in *On Feminist Ethics and Politics*, ed. Claudia Card (Lawrence: University Press of

Kansas, 1999), pp. 29–51; Marnia Lazreg, *The Eloquence of Silence: Algerian Women in Question* (New York: Routledge, 1994).

2. Kimberlé Crenshaw, "Mapping the Margins: Intersectionality, Identity Politics, and Violence against Women of Color," *Stanford Law Review* 43, 6 (1991): 1241–99; Patricia Hill Collins, *Black Feminist Thought* (Boston: Unwin Hyman, 1990); Maria Lugones and Elizabeth V. Spelman, "Have We Got a Theory for You! Feminist Theory, Cultural Imperialism, and the Demand for 'The Woman's Voice,'" in *Women and Values*, ed. Marilyn Pearsall (Belmont, Calif.: Wadsworth, 1999), pp. 14–24; Gloria Anzaldua, *La Conciencia de la Mestiza*: Towards a New Consciousness, in *Feminism and "Race,"* ed. Kum-Kum Bhavnani (Oxford: Oxford University Press, 2001), pp. 93–107.

3. See chapter 5.

4. Peter French, "The Corporation as a Moral Person," *American Philosophical Quarterly* 16, 3 (1979): 207: 15, reprinted in *Collective Responsibility*, ed. Larry May and Stacey Hoffman (Savage, Md.: Rowman and Littlefield, 1991), pp. 133–49.

5. Ibid., p. 145.

6. See Michael Bratman, *Faces of Intention: Selected Essays on Intention and Agency* (Cambridge: Cambridge University Press, 1999), and Christopher Kutz, *Complicity* (Cambridge: Cambridge University Press, 2001).

7. Searle analyzes collective intentions in this way, offering it, however, as a nonreductionism of sorts. It is nonreductionist insofar as he believes collective intentions of the form "we intend to do such-and-such" are not analyzable in terms of individual intentions of the form "I intend to do such-and-such." See his "Collective Intentions and Actions" in *Intentions in Communication*, ed. Philip R. Cohen, Jerry Morgan, and Martha E. Pollack (Cambridge, Mass.: MIT Press, 1990), pp. 401–15.

8. See Kutz, *Complicity*, p. 71.

9. Seumas Miller, *Social Action* (Cambridge: Cambridge University Press, 2001), p. 10.

10. Ibid., p. 58.

11. Raimo Tuomela, *The Philosophy of Sociality* (Oxford: Oxford University Press, 2007), p. 120.

12. Ibid., p. 19.

13. "The Wave" is a popular activity among fans at sports events with large crowds seated in stadiums or arenas in North America. It begins with the people in one section standing up at the same time, throwing their arms in the air, and cheering. Next, the people in the section beside them do it, and then in the section beside them, and so on. As each section jumps up and then sits down, the appearance is produced of a wave moving through the stands.

14. Michael Bratman, "Shared Intention," in *Faces of Intention: Selected Essays on Intention and Agency* (Cambridge: Cambridge University Press, 1999), pp. 109–29.

15. Ibid., p. 129.
16. Miller, *Social Action*, p. 33.
17. Other constraints on collective intention will be made clear later in this chapter.
18. I will have more to say about genocide as a special case later. For its articulation in international law, see Convention on the Prevention and Punishment of the Crime of Genocide.
19. See Kutz, *Complicity*, pp. 74–89.
20. Tuomela, *Philosophy of Sociality*, p. 84.
21. Ibid.
22. Bratman, "Shared Intention," and "I Intend That We J," in *Faces of Intention*, pp. 142–61.
23. Kutz, *Complicity*, p. 90.
24. Ibid., p. 90.
25. Ibid., p. 92.
26. Margaret Gilbert, "Walking Together: A Paradigmatic Social Phenomenon," *Midwest Studies in Philosophy* 15 (1990): 1–14, 3.

Chapter 2: Collective Moral Responsibility

1. And more than that, in international law "acts of genocide" are performed by individuals. These are not necessarily acts in which a genocide is completed, but rather, they are acts performed with a genocidal intent.
2. Chapter 4.
3. A look at genocide statutes in international law reveals a different understanding of it, tailored for the purpose of prosecuting individuals, not only collectives such as states, for genocide. Rather than seeing it as essentially or even usually collective on the side of the perpetrator, Article II of the United Nations' Convention on the Prevention and Punishment of the Crime of Genocide defines genocide as follows:

   any of the following acts committed with intent to destroy, in whole or in part, a national, ethnical, racial or religious group, as such:

   (a) Killing members of the group;
   (b) Causing serious bodily or mental harm to members of the group;
   (c) Deliberately inflicting on the group conditions of life calculated to bring about its physical destruction in whole or in part;
   (d) Imposing measures intended to prevent births within the group;
   (e) Forcibly transferring children of the group to another group.

   According to this statute, a single act is genocide if it is done with a particular intent, that is, the intent to destroy, in whole *or in part*, a particular kind of group. Understood in the terms of this Convention, genocide does not need to aim at the total annihilation of a group; it is enough that the destruction of even a part of a group be the intention behind the act. My point here is that, regardless of the individualistic possibilities for acts of genocide that the Convention affords, we can draw a useful distinction between an act of genocide and genocide itself, perhaps understood as *a* genocide.

4. H. D. Lewis, "Collective Responsibility," (1948), in *Collective Responsibility*, ed. Larry May and Stacey Hoffman (Savage, Md.: Rowman and Littlefield, 1991), pp. 17–33.

5. H. D. Lewis raises this concern. See ibid.

6. Attributed to Edward Thurlow (1731–1806), First Baron of Thurlow and lord chancellor of Great Britain under four different prime ministers.

7. See the collection Tracy Isaacs and Richard Vernon, eds., *Accountability for Collective Wrongdoing* (New York: Cambridge University Press, 2011).

8. Jan Narveson, "Collective Responsibility," *Journal of Ethics* 6, 2 (2002): 179–98, p. 185.

9. Ibid., p. 28.

10. Chapter 8 presents a more in-depth discussion of this difficulty.

11. John Searle places the following adequacy condition on collective intentionality: "It must be consistent with the fact that society consists of nothing but individuals. Since society consists entirely of individuals, there cannot be a group mind or group consciousness. All consciousness is in individual minds, in individual brains"; "Collective Intentions and Actions," in *Intentions in Communication*, ed. Phillip R. Cohen, Jerry Morgan, and Martha E. Pollack (Cambridge, Mass.: MIT Press, 1990), pp. 401–15, p. 406.

12. Narveson, "Collective Responsibility," p. 182.

13. Ibid., p. 180.

14. Ibid., p. 183.

Chapter 3: Collective Guilt

1. An anonymous referee for the Canadian Philosophical Association 2006 program noted the significance of this possibility.

2. See Karl Jaspers, *The Question of German Guilt*, trans. E. B. Ashton (New York: Capricorn Books, 1961 [1947]); Larry May, "Metaphysical Guilt and Moral Taint," in *Collective Responsibility*, ed. Larry May and Stacey Hoffman (Savage, Md.: Rowman and Littlefield, 1991), pp. 239–54.

3. See, for example, the extensive literature about the Trolley Problem and the difference between killing and letting die. Both discussions challenge the intuition that "killing is worse than letting die" or, more generally, that we are "more

responsible" for what we do than for what we allow to happen. Selected classic contributions to these discussions include Judith Jarvis Thompson, "Killing, Letting Die, and the Trolley Problem," *Monist* 59, 2 (1976): 204–17, and "The Trolley Problem," *Yale Law Journal* 94 (1985): 1395–415; Phillipa Foot, "The Problem of Abortion and the Doctrine of the Double Effect," in Foot, *Virtues and Vices and Other Essays in Moral Philosophy* (Oxford: Blackwell, 1978), pp. 19–32; Warren Quinn, "Actions, Intentions, and Consequences: The Doctrine of Doing and Allowing," *Philosophical Review* 98, 3 (July 1989): 287–312; Jonathan Bennett, "Whatever the Consequences," *Analysis* 63 (1966): 83–102; Frances Kamm, *Morality, Mortality*, vol. 2 (Oxford: Oxford University Press, 1996).

4. Sandra Bartky, "In Defence of Guilt," in *Feminist Ethics and Politics*, ed. Claudia Card (Lawrence: University Press of Kansas, 1999), pp. 30–51; p. 49.

5. Hannah Arendt, "Organized Guilt and Universal Responsibility," in *The Portable Hannah Arendt*, ed. Peter Baehr (New York: Penguin Books, 2000), p. 154.

6. Not everyone believes that the availability of choices or the ability to choose otherwise is essential to moral responsibility. See Harry Frankfurt, "Alternate Possibilities and Moral Responsibility," *Journal of Philosophy* 66 (1969): 829–39; Peter Strawson, "Freedom and Resentment," in *Free Will*, 2nd ed., ed. Gary Watson (Oxford: Oxford University Press, 2003), pp. 72–93.

7. Marilyn Frye, "White Woman Feminist," in *Overcoming Racism and Sexism*, ed. Linda Bell and David Blumfield (Savage, Md.: Rowman and Littlefield, 1983), pp. 113–34.

8. Chapter 6.

9. Jaspers, *Question of German Guilt*, p. 36.

10. A. Zvie Bar-on, "Measuring Responsibility," in May and Hoffman, *Collective Responsibility*, pp. 255–71.

11. See H. D. Lewis, "Collective Responsibility," in May and Hoffman, *Collective Responsibility*, pp. 17–33, and Jan Narveson, "Collective Responsibility," *Journal of Ethics* 6, 2 (2002): 179–98.

12. Chris MacDonald made this point in his comments on an earlier version of this chapter, presented at the annual meeting of the Canadian Philosophical Association, Toronto, June 1, 2006.

13. See the collection Nyla R. Branscombe and Bertjan Doosje, eds., *Collective Guilt: International Perspectives* (Cambridge: Cambridge University Press, 2005).

14. John Coffee Jr., in "No Soul to Damn, No Body to Kick: An Unscandalized Inquiry into the Problem of Corporate Punishment," *Michigan Law Review* 9, 3 (January 1981): 386–459, attributes to Edward, First Baron Thurlow (1731–1806), lord chancellor of England, the question "Did you ever expect a corporation to have a conscience, when it has no soul to be damned, and no body to be kicked?"

15. Nyla R. Branscombe and Bertjan Doosje, "International Perspectives on the Experience of Collective Guilt," chap. 1 of Branscombe and Doosje, *Collective Guilt*, pp. 3–15.

16. Margaret Gilbert, "Collective Guilt and Collective Guilt Feelings," *Journal of Ethics* 6 (2002): 115–43, p. 118.

17. Ibid., p. 126.

18. Ibid., p. 139.

19. Ibid., p. 139.

20. Ibid., p. 139.

21. Ibid., p. 118.

22. She says, for example: "Evidently collective guilt feelings—on the plural subject account—provide an analogue of personal guilt, at the collective level" (ibid., p. 140).

23. Thomas Hurka brought this point to my attention in the discussion period following the presentation of an earlier version of this chapter at the annual meeting of the Canadian Philosophical Association, Toronto, June 1, 2006.

Chapter 4: Individual Responsibility for (and in) Collective Wrongs

1. See Donald Davidson, *Essays on Actions and Events* (Oxford: Clarendon Press, 1980).

2. Donald Davidson, "Agency" and "The Individuation of Events," in ibid., pp. 43–61 and 163–180.

3. As cited by Davidson in "Agency," p. 53.

4. See Bernard Williams, *Ethics and the Limits of Philosophy* (Cambridge, Mass.: Harvard University Press, 1985).

5. André Picard, *The Gift of Death* (Toronto: HarperCollins, 1995), p. 232.

6. Ibid., p. 233.

7. Ibid., p. 233.

8. Ibid., p. 248.

9. Larry May, *Crimes against Humanity: A Normative Account* (Cambridge: Cambridge University Press, 2005).

10. Factor concentrate is a "concentrated form of blood factors, most commonly Factor VIII and Factor IX [both of which are required for clotting]; small vials of white powder to be reconstituted with distilled water. Vials contain between 200 and 1,200 international units; a moderate hemophiliac requires about 40,000 international units annually" (Picard, *Gift of Death*, 275). Because one "batch" was made from the plasma of many donors, the blood of one infected donor would infect countless units of factor concentrate.

11. May, *Crimes against Humanity*, p. 154.
12. Phillip Petit, "Responsibility Incorporated," *Ethics* 117 (January 2007): 171–201.
13. Christopher Kutz, *Complicity* (Cambridge: Cambridge University Press, 2001), 162.
14. Kutz, *Complicity*, 141.
15. Seumas Miller, *Social Action: A Teleological Account* (Cambridge: Cambridge University Press, 2001), p. 248.
16. Kutz, *Complicity*, 122.

Chapter 5: Collective Obligation, Individual Obligation, and Individual Moral Responsibility

1. I owe this point to Brian Lawson.
2. H. D. Lewis, "Collective Responsibility," in *Collective Responsibility*, ed. Larry May and Stacey Hoffman (Savage, Md.: Rowman and Littlefield, 1991), pp. 17–33.
3. Anthony Skelton raised this objection.
4. For a fuller discussion of the effectiveness of collective action see my "Feminism and Agency," in *Feminist Moral Philosophy*, ed. Samantha Brennan, *Canadian Journal of Philosophy*, supp. vol. 28 (Calgary: University of Calgary Press, 2003), pp. 129–54.
5. Peter French, "Types of Collectives," in *Individual and Collective Responsibility*, 2nd ed., ed. Peter French (Rochester, Vt.: Schenkman Books, 1998), pp. 33–50.
6. Larry May, "Collective Inaction and Responsibility," in French, *Individual and Collective Responsibility*, pp. 211–31; p. 218.
7. David Copp, "Responsibility and Collective Inaction," in French, *Individual and Collective Responsibility*, pp. 233–49.
8. Virginia Held, "Can a Random Collection of Individuals Be Morally Responsible?," in May and Hoffman, *Collective Responsibility*, pp. 89–100, p. 98.
9. Ibid., p. 94.
10. Ibid.

Chapter 6: Moral Responsibility in Wrongful Social Practice

Many of the ideas discussed in this chapter can be found in my article "Cultural Context and Moral Responsibility," *Ethics* 107 (July 1997): 670–84.

1. Cheshire Calhoun, "Responsibility and Reproach," *Ethics* 99 (1989): 389–409, p. 389.
2. Susan Wolf, "Sanity and the Metaphysics of Responsibility," in *Responsibility, Character, and the Emotions: New Essays in Moral Psychology*, ed. Ferdinand Schoeman (Cambridge: Cambridge University Press, 1987), pp. 46–61, and *Freedom within Reason* (New York: Oxford University Press, 1990).
3. Michele Moody-Adams, "Culture, Responsibility, and Affected Ignorance," *Ethics* 104 (1994): 291–309.
4. Ibid., p. 296.
5. Ibid.
6. Owen Flanagan, *Varieties of Moral Personality: Ethics and Psychological Realism* (Cambridge, Mass.: Harvard University Press, 1993), pp. 300–301.
7. I owe this point to Michael Milde.
8. Calhoun, "Responsibility and Reproach," p. 394.
9. Ibid., p. 396.
10. Here it will be necessary to examine empirically the potential for individuals to acquire new perspectives, and the psychological limits facing them. Evidence from our ordinary experience suggests that shifts in perspective are possible. Ultimately, empirical evidence documenting the potential for and limits of this kind of perceptual shift ought to be consulted. But realism and optimism both suggest that human agents have a great deal of potential in this area, though it is obviously not easy for us to make these changes.
11. Calhoun, "Responsibility and Reproach," p. 402.
12. Ibid., p. 405.
13. Ibid., p. 405.
14. Ibid., p. 390.
15. This difficulty was raised in a very helpful way by Eric Lewis in the discussion period following my presentation of this work at McGill University.
16. Violetta Igneski first brought this concern to my attention.
17. For a dissenting opinion about the prevalence of coercive conditions, see Daniel Jonah Goldhagen, *Hitler's Willing Executioners: Ordinary Germans and the Holocaust* (New York: Vintage Books, 1997). Goldhagen argues that most ordinary Germans were not ignorant of the Holocaust and that those who participated did so willingly, not, as the received view would have it, reluctantly and out of fear of the consequences of not participating.
18. Compare Thomas Nagel's discussion of "luck in circumstances" in "Moral Luck," in his *Mortal Questions* (Cambridge: Cambridge University Press, 1979), pp. 24–38.
19. Discussions of this distinction occur, not exclusively, in Peter Railton, "Alienation, Consequentialism, and the Demands of Morality," *Philosophy and Public Affairs* 13 (1984): 134–71; W. D. Ross, *The Right and the Good* (Oxford: Oxford University Press, 1930); Henry Sidgwick, *The Methods of Ethics*, 7th ed. (1907; reprint, Indianapolis: Hackett, 1981), pp. 207–10.

Conclusion

1. Loren Fox, *Enron: the Rise and Fall* (Hoboken, N.J.: Wiley, 2003); Alex Gibney, Jason Kliot, and Susan Motamed, producers, *Enron: the Smartest Guys in the Room* (Los Angeles: Magnolia Home Entertainment, 2006), videorecording; Theodore F. Sterling, ed., *The Enron Scandal* (Hauppage, N.Y.: Nova Science, 2002).

2. In 1984 a gas and chemical leak occurred at the Union Carbide pesticide plant in Bhopal, India. According to Amnesty International, over half a million people were exposed and "between 7,000 and 10,000 people died in the immediate aftermath and a further 15,000 over the next 20 years." See Amnesty International, "First Convictions for 1984 Union Carbide Disaster in Bhopal Too Little, Too Late," June 7, 2010, www.amnesty.org/en/news-and-updates/first-convictions-1984-union-carbide-disaster-bhopal-too-little-too-late-2010-06-07.

3. Jean M. Bartunek, Mary Ann Hinsdale, and James F. Keenan, eds., *Church Ethics in Its Organizational Context: Learning from the Sex Abuse Scandal in the Catholic Church* (Lanham, Md.: Rowman and Littlefield, 2006).

4. "BPs Insurance Will Mitigate Oil Spill Liability: Analyst," *Financial Post*, August 31, 2010, http://business.financialpost.com/2010/08/31/bps-insurance-will-mitigate-oil-spill-liability-analyst/.

5. "Toyota Announces Massive Recall," *Toronto Star*, January 22, 2010, www.thestar.com/business/article/754130—toyota-announces-massive-recall.

6. See Mark Drumbl, *Atrocity, Punishment, and International Law* (New York: Cambridge University Press, 2007); Tracy Isaacs and Richard Vernon, eds., *Accountability for Collective Wrongdoing* (New York: Cambridge University Press, 2011); Martha Minow, *Between Vengeance and Forgiveness: Facing History after Genocide and Mass Violence* (Boston: Beacon Press, 1998).

BIBLIOGRAPHY

Anzaldua, Gloria. *La conciencia de la Mestiza*: Towards a New Consciousness." In *Feminism and "Race,"* ed. Kum-Kum Bhavnani (Oxford: Oxford University Press, 2001), pp. 93–107.

Bar-on, A. Zvie. "Measuring Responsibility." In May and Hoffman 1991, pp. 255–71.

Bartky, Sandra. "In Defence of Guilt." In *Feminist Ethics and Politics*, ed. Claudia Card (Lawrence: University Press of Kansas, 1999), pp. 30–51.

Branscombe, Nyla R., and Bertjan Doosje, eds. *Collective Guilt: International Perspectives* (Cambridge: Cambridge University Press, 2005).

———. "International Perspectives on the Experience of Collective Guilt." Chapter 1 of Branscombe and Doosje 2005, pp. 3–15.

Bratman, Michael. *Faces of Intention: Selected Essays on Intention and Agency* (Cambridge: Cambridge University Press, 1999).

———. "Shared Cooperative Activity." *Philosophical Review* 101, 2 (1992): 327–41.

———. "Shared Intention." *Ethics* 104 (1993): 97–113.

———. "Two Faces of Intention." *Philosophical Review* 93, 3 (July 1984): 375–405.

Calhoun, Cheshire. "Responsibility and Reproach." *Ethics* 99 (1989): 389–406.

Coffee, John, Jr. "No Soul to Damn, No Body to Kick: An Unscandalized Inquiry into the Problem of Corporate Punishment." *Michigan Law Review* 9, 3 (January 1981):386–459.

Collins, Patricia Hill. *Black Feminist Thought* (Boston: Unwin Hyman, 1990).

Cooper, D. E. "Collective Responsibility." In May and Hoffman 1991, pp. 35–51.

Copp, David. "On the Agency of Certain Collective Entities: An Argument from 'Normative Autonomy.'" In French 2006, pp. 194–221.

———. "Responsibility and Collective Inaction." In French 1998, pp. 233–49.

————. "What Collectives Are: Agency, Individualism, and Legal Theory." *Dialogue* 23 (1984): 249–69.

Crenshaw, Kimberlé. "Mapping the Margins: Intersectionality, Identity Politics, and Violence against Women of Color." *Stanford Law Review* 43, 6 (1991): 1241–299.

Dallaire, Roméo. *Shake Hands with the Devil* (Toronto: Random House, 2003).

Darley, John M., and Bibb Latane. "Bystander Intervention in Emergencies: Diffusion of Responsibility." *Journal of Personality and Social Psychology* 8 (1968): 377–83.

Davidson, Donald. *Essays on Actions and Events* (Oxford: Clarendon Press, 1980).

Eltringham, Nigel. *Accounting for Horror: Post-genocide Debates in Rwanda* (London: Pluto Press, 2004).

Feinberg, Joel. "Action and Responsibility." In *Philosophy in America*, ed. M. Black (Ithaca, N.Y.: Cornell University Press, 1965), pp. 134–60.

Flanagan, Owen. *Varieties of Moral Personality: Ethics and Psychological Realism* (Cambridge, Mass.: Harvard University Press, 1993)

Frankfurt, Harry. "Alternate Possibilities and Moral Responsibility." *Journal of Philosophy* 66 (1969): 829–39.

French, Peter. "The Corporation as a Moral Person." *American Philosophical Quarterly* 16, 3 (1979): 207–15.

————, ed. *Individual and Collective Responsibility* (Rochester, Vt.: Schenkman Books, 1998).

————, ed. *Midwest Studies in Philosophy*, vol. 30, Theme: Shared Intentions and Collective Responsibility, editor (Oxford: Blackwell Publishing Inc., 2006.

————, ed. "Types of Collectivities." In French 1998, pp. 33–50.

Gilbert, Margaret. "Collective Guilt and Collective Guilt Feelings." *Journal of Ethics* 6 (2002): 115–43.

————. *Sociality and Responsibility* (Lanham, Md.: Rowman and Littlefield, 2000).

————. "Walking Together: A Paradigmatic Social Phenomenon." *Midwest Studies in Philosophy* 15 (1990): 1–14.

————. "What Is It for *Us* to Intend?" In Tuomela and Holmstrom-Hintikka 1997, pp. 65–85.

Gildert, Robin. "Acknowledging Genocide: A Retributivist Account of Collective Moral Responsibility." Paper presented at the annual meeting of Concerned Philosophers for Peace, McMaster University, Hamilton, Ontario, October 26–29, 2000.

Gilligan, Carol. *In a Different Voice* (Cambridge, Mass.: Harvard University Press, 1982).

Goodin, Robert. *Utilitarianism as a Public Philosophy* (Cambridge: Cambridge University Press, 1995.

Gourevitch, Philip. *We Wish to Inform You That Tomorrow We Will Be Killed with Our Families: Stories from Rwanda* (New York: Farrar, Straus and Giroux, 1998).

Green, Leslie. "Legal Obligation and Authority." In *The Stanford Encyclopedia of Philosophy*, spring 2004, ed. Edward N. Zalta, http://plato.stanford.edu/archives/spr2004/entires/legal-obligation/.

Guyer, Paul. "Kant, Immanuel." In *Routledge Encyclopedia of Philosophy*, ed. E. Craig (London: Routledge, 2004), www.rep.routledge.com/article/DB047SECT10, accessed February 10, 2006.

Held, Virginia. "Can a Random Collection of Individuals Be Morally Responsible?" In May and Hoffman 1991, pp. 89–100.

Isaacs, Tracy. "Collective Intention and Collective Moral Responsibility." In "Shared Intention and Collective Responsibility," special issue, *Midwest Studies in Philosophy*, ed. Peter French (2006): 59–73.

———. "Cultural Context and Moral Responsibility." *Ethics* 107, 4 (July 1997): 670–84.

———. "Domestic Violence and Hate Crimes: Two Levels of Responsibility." *Criminal Justice Ethics* 20, 2 (summer/fall 2001): 31–43.

———. "Feminism and Agency." In *Feminist Moral Theory*, ed. Samantha Brennan, *Canadian Journal of Philosophy* supp. vol. 28 (Calgary: University of Calgary Press, 2003), pp. 129–54.

———. "Individual Responsibility for Collective Wrongs." In *Bringing Power to Justice*, ed. Joanna Harrington, Michael Milde, and Richard Vernon (Montreal: McGill-Queen's University Press, 2006), pp. 267–308.

———. "Moral Theory and Action Theory, Killing and Letting Die." *American Philosophical Quarterly* 32, 4 (October 1995): 355–68.

Jaspers, Karl. *The Question of German Guilt*. Trans. E. B. Ashton (1947; reprint, New York: Capricorn Books, 1961).

Kant, Immanuel. *Grounding for the Metaphysics of Morals*. Trans. James W. Ellington (Indianapolis: Hackett, 1981). (Originally published in 1785)

Kutz, Christopher. *Complicity: Ethics and Law for a Collective Age* (Cambridge: Cambridge University Press, 2000).

Lazreg, Marnia. *The Eloquence of Silence: Algerian Women in Question* (New York: Routledge, 1994).

Lewis, H. D. "Collective Responsibility." In May and Hoffman 1991, pp. 17–33.

Lugones, Maria, and Elizabeth V. Spelman. "Have We Got a Theory for You! Feminist Theory, Cultural Imperialism, and the Demand for 'The Woman's Voice.'" In *Women and Values*, ed. Marilyn Pearsall (Belmont, Calif.: Wadsworth, 1999), pp. 14–24.

May, Larry. "Collective Inaction and Responsibility." In French 1998, pp. 211–31.

———. *Crime against Humanity: A Normative Account* (Cambridge University Press, 2005).

———. "Metaphysical Guilt and Moral Taint." In May and Hoffman 1991, pp. 239–54.

———. *The Morality of Groups* (Notre Dame, Ind.: University of Notre Dame Press, 1987).

———. *Sharing Responsibility* (Chicago: University of Chicago Press, 1992).

May, Larry, and Stacey Hoffman, eds. *Collective Responsibility: Five Decades of Debate in Theoretical and Applied Ethics* (Savage, Md.: Rowman and Littlefield, 1991).

McIntosh, Peggy. "White Privilege and Male Privilege: A Personal Account of Coming to See Correspondences through Work in Women's Studies," Working Paper 189 (Wellesley, Mass.: Wellesley College Center for Research on Women, 1988), pp. 24–38.

Mellema, Gregory. *Collective Responsibility* (Amsterdam: Rodopi Press, 1997).

Miller, Seumas. *On Social Action* (Cambridge: Cambridge University Press, 2001).

Mohanty, Chandra. *Feminism without Borders* (Durham, N.C.: Duke University Press, 2003).

Moody-Adams, Michelle. "Culture, Responsibility, and Affected Ignorance." *Ethics* 104 (1994): 291–309.

Nagel, Thomas. "Moral Luck." In *Mortal Questions* (Cambridge: Cambridge University Press, 1979), pp. 24–38.

Narayan, Uma. *Dislocating Cultures: Identities, Traditions, and Third World Feminism* (New York: Routledge, 1997).

Narveson, Jan. "Collective Responsibility." *Journal of Ethics* 6, 2 (2002): 179–98.

Pettit, Philip. "Groups with Minds of Their Own." In *Socializing Metaphysics: The Nature of Social Reality*, ed. Frederick Schmidtt (Lanham, Md.: Rowman and Littlefield, 2003), pp. 167–93.

Picard, André. *The Gift of Death: Confronting Canada's Tainted-Blood Tragedy* (Toronto: HarperCollins Publishers Ltd., 1995).

Railton, Peter. "Alienation, Consequentialism, and the Demands of Morality." *Philosophy and Public Affairs* 13 (1984): 134–71.

Ross, W. D. *The Right and the Good* (Oxford: Oxford University Press, 1930).

Searle, John. "Collective Intentions and Action." In *Intentions in Communication*, ed. Philip R. Cohen, J. Morgan, and M. E. Pollack (Cambridge, Mass.: MIT Press, 1990), pp. 401–15.

Sidgwick, Henry. *The Methods of Ethics.* 7th ed. (1907; reprint, Indianapolis: Hackett, 1981).

Singer, Peter. "Famine, Affluence and Morality." *Philosophy and Public Affairs* 1, 1 (spring 1972): 229–43.

Strawson, Peter. "Freedom and Resentment." In *Free Will*, 2nd ed., ed. Gary Watson (Oxford University Press, 2003), pp. 72–93.

Taraku, Sylo. *Prosecuting Genocide in Rwanda: The Gacaca System and the International Criminal Tribunal for Rwanda.* Report II/2002. (Oslo: Norweigian Helskini Committee for Human Rights, 2002).

Tuomela, Raimo. "From Social Imitation to Teamwork." In Tuomela and Holmstrom-Hintikka 1997, pp. 1–47.

———. *The Importance of Us* (Stanford, Calif.: Stanford University Press, 1995).

———. *The Philosophy of Sociality* (Oxford: Oxford University Press, 2007).

————. "We Will Do It: An Analysis of Group-Intentions." *Philosophy and Phenomenological Research* 51, 2 (June 1991): 249–77.

Tuomela, Raino, and Maj Bonnevier-Tuomela. *Contemporary Action Theory.* Vol. 2 (Boston: Kluwer Academic, 1997).

Velleman, David. "How to Share an Intention." *Philosophy and Phenomenological Research* 57, 1 (March 1997): 29–50.

Watson, Gary. Introduction to Watson 2003, pp. 1–15.

————. *Free Will.* 2nd ed. (Oxford: Oxford University Press, 2003).

Wolf, Susan. "Sanity and the Metaphysics of Responsibility." In Watson 2003, pp. 372–87.

INDEX

abnormal moral contexts, 161, 164–73,
181; knowledge-acquiring subgroups in,
165–66, 170–71, 191n10; reproach and
dialogue in, 168–73
accordion effects, 101–2, 106, 124–25, 180
acquisition of new perspectives, 166, 191n10
action descriptions, 100–102, 106–7,
124–25
action-intentions, 39
affected ignorance, 161–64, 174
aggregates, 26–27
aim-intentions, 39
Arendt, Hannah, 78
Asch, Solomon, 162–63
authority structures, 97–98

Bartky, Sandra, 78
bindingness, 48–49
blameworthiness, 15–16, 18, 53, 55, 130,
177; in collective wrongdoing, 102–3;
punishment for, 62–64, 181, 187n6;
reification of abstract entities in, 66;
in understandings of guilt, 71–74, 76,
81–82, 93; for wrongful social practices,
174, 175. See also collective guilt
Branscombe, Nyla R., 85

Bratman, Michael, 36; on common
knowledge, 42; on joint intentional
action, 39–41
bystanders, 77–78, 187n3; coordinated
obligations of, 143–44, 153; individual
obligations of, 141–43

Calhoun, Cheshire: on normal and abnormal
moral contexts, 161, 164–67; on reproach
and dialogue, 168–69, 172–73
Canadian Red Cross blood supply case, 4,
25, 27, 103–5, 177–78; individual and
collective agency in, 105–7, 189n10;
intentional structures of, 28–29
causal responsibility, 13–14
clarity of obligation: in abnormal moral contexts, 166–68; reasonable person standard
of, 148–53, 156–57, 166–67; transition
from ignorance to, 161, 163–64, 167–76,
191n10
collective agency, 23–51, 178–81;
bindingness in, 48–49; collective guilt
in, 82–83; collective intention in, 36–38,
66–67, 187n11; common knowledge
requirements in, 41–45; compromise
in, 30; degrees of collectivity in, 45–48;